6
JUNIOR
CLASSICS

Published in Red Turtle by
Rupa Publications India Pvt. Ltd 2016
7/16, Ansari Road, Daryaganj
New Delhi 110002

Sales centres:
Allahabad Bengaluru Chennai
Hyderabad Jaipur Kathmandu
Kolkata Mumbai

Edition copyright © Rupa Publications India Pvt. Ltd. 2016

All rights reserved.
No part of this publication may be reproduced, transmitted, or stored in a retrieval system, in any form or by any means, electronic, mechanical, photocopying, recording or otherwise, without the prior permission of the publisher.

ISBN: 978-81-291-3890-3

First impression 2016

10 9 8 7 6 5 4 3 2 1

This book is sold subject to the condition that it shall not, by way of trade or otherwise, be lent, resold, hired out, or otherwise circulated, without the publisher's prior consent, in any form of binding or cover other than that in which it is published.

Contents

The Mutiny of the *Bounty* (*John Barrow*)   4

The Adventures of Pinocchio
(*Carlo Collodi*)   32

King Solomon's Mines (*H. Rider Haggard*)   66

20,000 Leagues under the Sea
(*Jules Verne*)   96

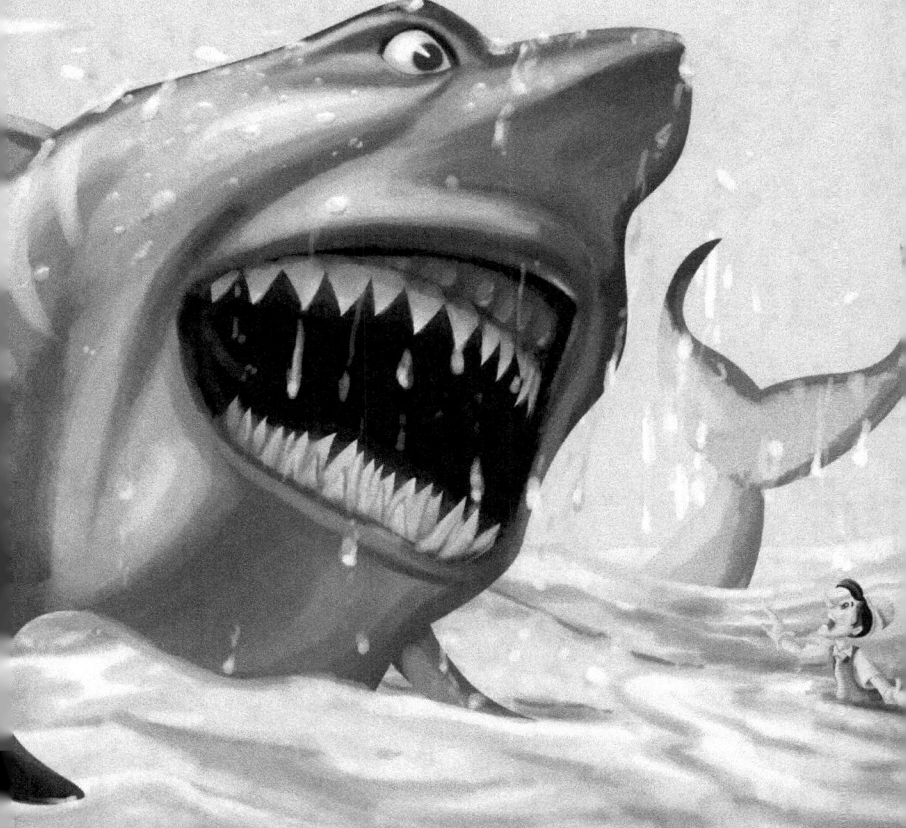

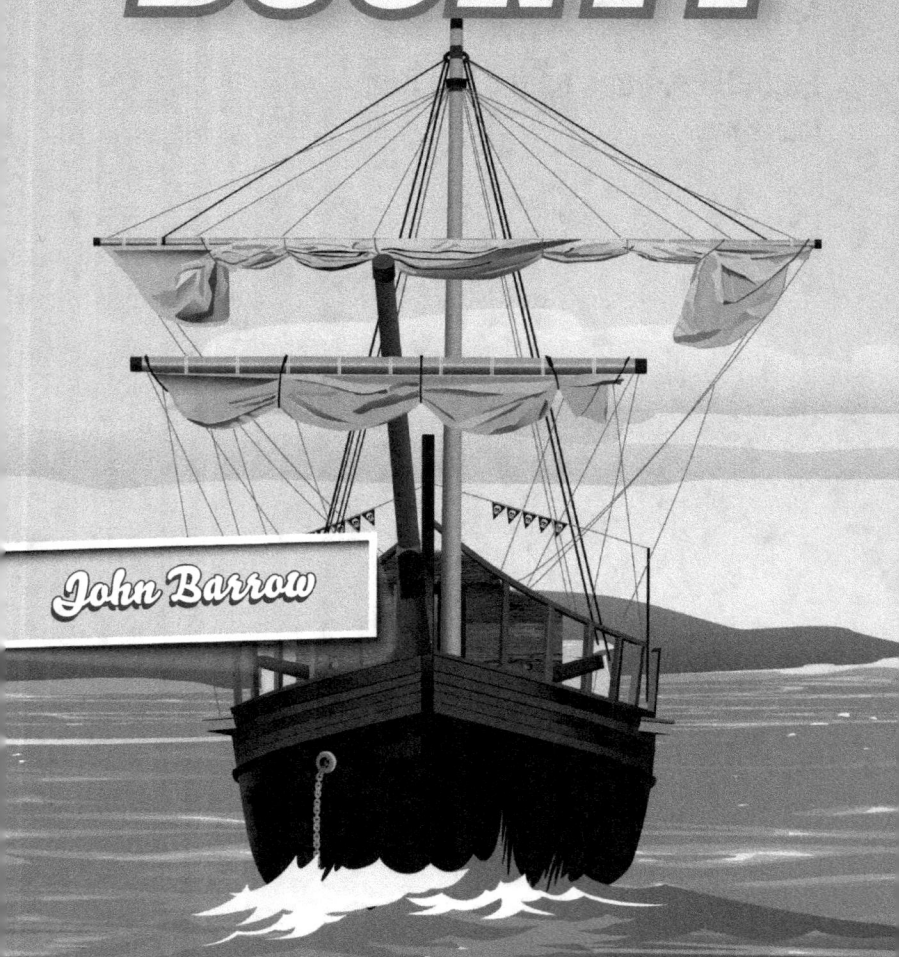

The Royal Society, in 1768, addressed an application to the king, requesting him to appoint a ship of war to the South Seas. Mr Alexander Dalrymple, and certain others, were to observe the transit of Venus over the sun's disc, which was to happen in 1769. But, as Mr Dalrymple was a civilian, he could not be entrusted with the command of the ship, and on that account declined going in her.

The command was therefore conferred on Lieutenant James Cook, an officer of undoubted ability. Cook was also well versed in astronomy as well as in the theory and practice of navigation. However, Captain Wallis returned from his expedition. He strongly recommended Port Royal Harbour, an island he had discovered, to which he had given the name of 'King George's Island.' It was earlier known by its native name, Otaheite or Tahite, as most suitable for the purpose.

In 1787, after Cook's return from his first voyage, the merchants and planters resident in London were interested in

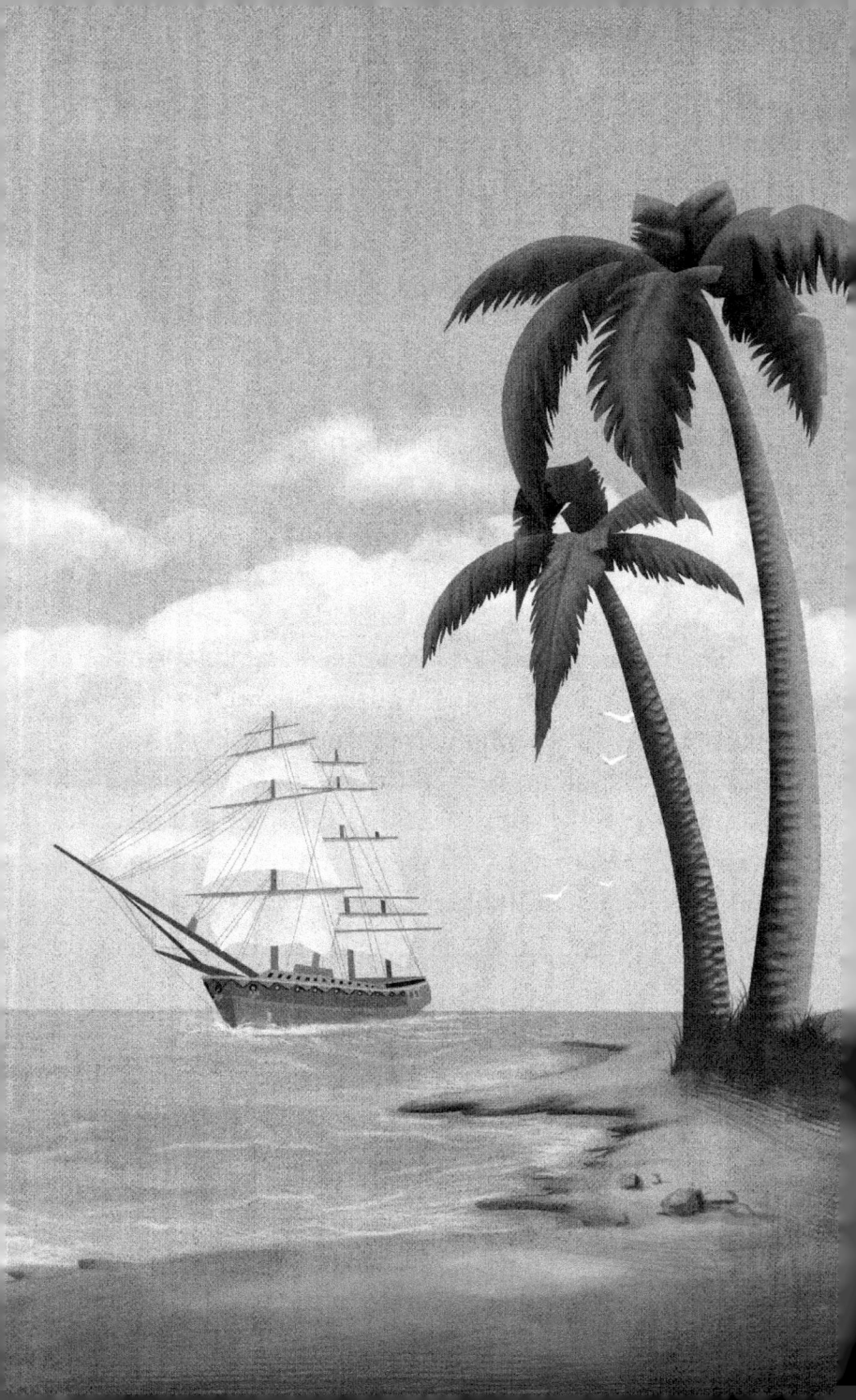

the West India possessions. They suggested to His Majesty, that the introduction of the breadfruit tree into the islands of those seas, to constitute an article of food. This would be of essential benefit to the inhabitants. The king was graciously pleased to comply with their request. A vessel was accordingly purchased, and fitted at Deptford with the necessary fixtures and preparations, for carrying it. The arrangements for disposing the plants were undertaken, and completed in the most effective manner by Sir Joseph Banks. He named the ship the *Bounty*, and recommended Lieutenant Bligh, who had been with Captain Cook, to command her.

Her burden was about two hundred and fifteen tons; and her establishment consisted of about forty-four. To this Sir Joseph Banks added two skilful and careful men, to have the management of the plants intended to be carried to the West Indies. Some other men were brought home for his Majesty's garden at Kew. One was David Nelson, who had served in a similar situation in Captain Cook's last voyage; the other William Brown, as an assistant to him.

The breadfruit plant was no new discovery of either Wallis or Cook. No object was deemed more likely to realize as beneficial than the breadfruit. It was hoped it might also do the same for the black population of the West India Islands.

On 23 December 1787, the *Bounty* sailed from Spithead, and on the 26th, it blew a severe storm of wind from the eastwards. The problem continued till the 29th, in the course of which the ship suffered greatly. One sea broke away the spare-yards and spars out of the starboard main-chains. Another heavy sea broke into the ship and destroyed all the boats. Several casks of beer that had been lashed upon deck, were broke loose and washed overboard. It was with great difficulty and risk that they were able to secure the boats from being washed away entirely. Besides, a large quantity of bread was damaged and rendered useless, for the sea had forced itself and filled the cabin with water.

This made it desirable to touch at Teneriffe, where they arrived on 5 January 1788, and having refitted and refreshed, they sailed again on the 10th.

'I now,' said Bligh, 'divided the people into three watches, and gave the charge of the third watch to Mr Fletcher Christian, one of the mates. I am persuaded that a complete rest not only contributes much towards the health of the ship's company, but enables them to exert themselves in cases of sudden emergency.'

On Sunday, 2 March, Lieutenant Bligh observed, 'After seeing that every person was clean, divine service was performed, according to my usual custom. On this day I gave to Mr Fletcher Christian, whom I had before desired to take charge of the third watch, a written order to act as lieutenant.'

Having reached as far as the latitude of 36 degree south, on 9 March, 'The change of temperature,' he observed, 'began to be sensibly felt; there being a variation in the thermometer, since yesterday, of eight degrees. That the people might not suffer by their own negligence, I gave orders for their light tropical clothing to be put on. I had also made them dress in a manner more suited to a cold climate. I had provided for this before I left England, by giving directions for such clothes to be purchased as would be found necessary. On this day, on a complaint of the master, I found it necessary to punish Matthew Quintal, one of the seamen, with two dozen lashes, for mutinous behaviour. Before this I had not had an occasion to punish any person on board.'

The sight of New Year's Harbour, in Staaten Land, almost tempted him to put in. But the pleasant weather and the company of so many friendly people made him patient. He decided to stay on until they reach Otaheite. They soon had to encounter tremendous weather off Cape Horn, storms of wind, with hail and sleet, which made it necessary to keep a constant fire night and day. One of them always had to attend to dry the people's wet clothes. This stormy weather continued for nine days; while the ship began to complain, and required pumping every hour. The decks became so leaky that the commander was obliged to allot the great cabin to those who had wet berths, to hang their hammocks in. They were losing ground every day. It was almost hopeless to persist in attempting a passage by this route, at this season of the year, to the Society Islands. After struggling for thirty days in that tempestuous ocean, they decided to head towards the Cape of Good Hope.

They arrived at the Cape on 23 May, remained there thirty-eight days to refit the ship, replenish provisions and refresh the crew. They sailed again on 1 July, and anchored in Adventure Bay, in Van Diemen's Land, on 20 August. Here they remained taking in wood and water till 4 September. After a month and a half, on the evening of 25 October they saw Otaheite.

On one occasion the *Bounty* had nearly gone ashore in a tremendous gale of wind, and on another did actually get aground. On both the occasions, the kind-hearted people of Otaheite came in groups to congratulate the captain on her escape. Many of them were stated to have been affected in the most lively manner, shedding tears while the ship was putting up against the harsh weather.

On 9 December, the surgeon of the *Bounty* died from the effects of heavy drinking and laziness. The doctor was always in a constant state of intoxication, and he hated any kind of exercise. Throughout the journey he was confined to one place and never did he go to the deck.

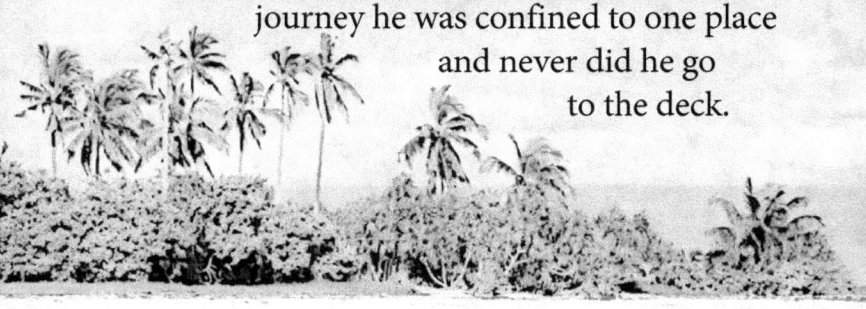

Lieutenant Bligh had obtained permission to bury him on shore; and ongoing with the chief Tinah to the spot intended for his burial place, 'I found,' said he, 'the natives had already begun to dig his grave. Tinah asked if they were doing it right?

'There,' said he, 'the sun rises, and there it sets.'

When the funeral took place, the chiefs and many of the natives attended the ceremony, and showed great attention during the service. Many of the principal natives attended divine service on Sundays, and behaved with great decency. Some of the women at one time betrayed an inclination to laugh at the general responses; but, the captain said, on looking at them they appeared much ashamed.

The *Bounty* arrived on 26 October 1788, and remained till 4 April 1789. On 31 March, the commander said, 'Today, all the plants were on board, being in seven hundred and seventy-four pots, thirty-nine tubs, and twenty-four boxes. The number of breadfruit plants were one thousand and fifteen; besides which, we had collected a number of other plants which Sir Joseph Banks recommended.'

While these active preparations for departure were going on, the good chief Tinah, on bringing a present for King George, could not refrain from shedding tears. During the remainder of their stay, there appeared among the natives an evident degree of sorrow that they were so soon to leave them. It was apparent from more than usual degree of their kindness and attention. Tinah, with his wife, brothers and sister requested permission to remain on board for the night previous to the sailing of the *Bounty*. The ship was crowded the whole day with the natives, and she was loaded with presents of coconuts, plantains, breadfruits, hogs and goats. Contrary to what had been the usual practice, there was this evening no dancing or mirth on the beach, such as they had long been accustomed to, but all was silent.

At sunset, the boat returned from landing Tinah and his wife, and the ship begun to sail, bidding farewell to Otaheite, where, Bligh observed, 'For twenty-three weeks we had been treated with the utmost affection and regard, and which seemed to increase in proportion to our stay.'

* * *

The following is Mr Bligh's account of the mutiny on the ship:

On the morning of 28 April, the northwesternmost of the Friendly Islands, called Tofoa, bearing northeast, I was steering to the westwards with a ship in most perfect order. On leaving the deck I gave directions for the course to be steered during the night. The master had the first watch; the gunner, the middle watch; and Mr Christian, the morning watch. This was the turn of duty for the night.

Just before the sunrise on Tuesday the 28th, while I was yet asleep—Mr Christian, officer of the watch, Charles Churchill, ship's corporal, John Mills, gunner's mate, and Thomas Burkitt, the seaman—came into my cabin, and seizing me, tied my hands with a cord behind my back. They threatened me with instant death if I spoke or made the least noise. I shouted, however, as loud as I could in hopes of assistance. However, they had already secured the officers who were not of their party, by placing the guards at their doors. There were three men at my cabin door, besides the four inside. Christian had only a cutlass in his hand, while the others had muskets and bayonets.

I was hauled out of bed, and forced on deck in my shirt, suffering great pain from the tightness with which they had tied my hands behind my back, held by Fletcher Christian, and Charles Churchill. The latter had a bayonet at my breast. Two other men, Alexander Smith and Thomas Burkitt were behind, with loaded muskets cocked and bayonets fixed. I demanded the reason of such violence, but received no other answer than abuse. The master, the gunner, Mr Elphinstone, the master's mate, and Nelson, were kept confined below; and the fore-hatchway was guarded by watchmen. The boatswain and carpenter, and also Mr Samuel the clerk, were allowed to come upon deck, where they saw me standing with my hands tied behind my back, under a guard, with Christian at their head. The boatswain was ordered to hoist the launch out, with a threat, if he did not do it instantly, to take care of himself.

When the boat was out, Mr Hayward and Mr Hallet, two of the midshipmen, and Mr Samuel, were ordered into it. I demanded what their intention was in giving this order. I tried to persuade the people near me not to indulge in such acts of violence. But it was to no effect—'Hold your tongue, Sir, or you are dead this instant,' was constantly repeated to me.

The master by this time had sent to request that he might come on deck, which was permitted. Yet he was soon ordered back again to his cabin.

When I exerted myself in speaking loud, to try if I could rally any with a sense of duty in them, I was saluted with—'d—n his eyes, the——, blow his brains out'; while Christian was threatening to kill me, if I did not hold my tongue.

I continued trying to turn the tide of affairs. When Christian changed the cutlass for a bayonet, and holding me with a strong grip by the cord that tied my hands, he threatened to kill me again, if I would not be quiet. The villains had their pieces cocked and bayonets fixed. Particular persons were called on to go into the boat and were hurried over the side. I concluded that with these people I was to be set adrift. I therefore made another effort to bring about a change, but with no other effect than to be threatened with having my brains blown out.

The boatswain and seamen who were to go in the boat, were allowed to collect twine, canvas, lines, sails, cordage, an eight-and-twenty gallon cask of water. Mr Samuel got one hundred and fifty pounds of bread, with a small quantity of rum and wine, also a quadrant and compass. However, he was forbidden to touch either map, ephemeris the book of astronomical observations, sextant, timekeeper, or any of my surveys or drawings.

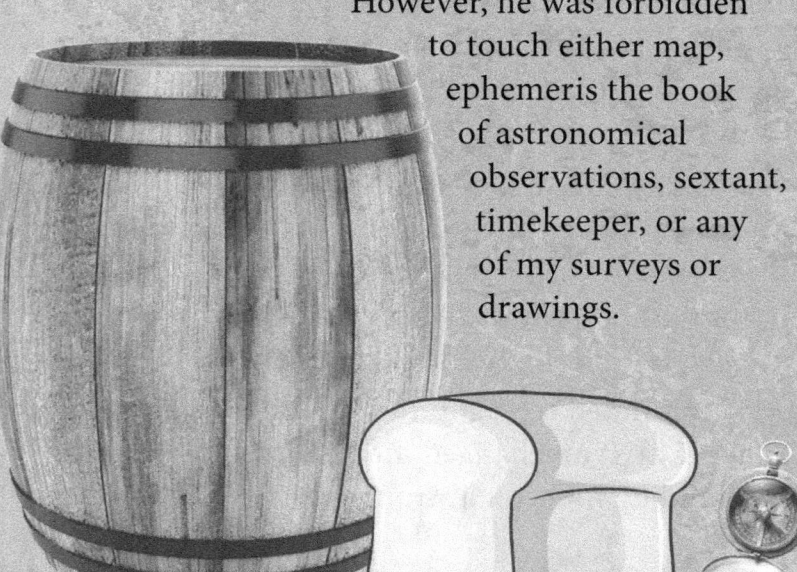

The mutineers having forced those of the seamen whom they meant to get rid of into the boat. Christian directed a dram to be served to each of his own crew. I then unhappily saw that nothing could be done to effect the recovery of the ship: there was no one to assist me, and every attempt on my part was answered with threats of death.

The officers were next called upon deck, and forced over the side into the boat, while I was kept apart from every one. Christian, armed with a bayonet, was holding me by the bandage that secured my hands. The guard had their pieces cocked, but on my daring the ungrateful rogues, as always, threatened to kill me.

Isaac Martin, one of the guards over me, had an inclination to assist me. As he fed me with shaddock (my lips being quite parched) we explained our wishes to each other by our looks. The other guards had observed us and Martin was soon dismissed from the room. He then attempted to leave the ship, for which purpose he got into the boat; but with many threats they asked him to return.

The armourer, Joseph Coleman, and two of the carpenters, M'Intosh and Norman, were also kept against their wishes. They begged of me, after I was astern in the boat, to remember that they declared they had no hand in the transaction. Michael Byrne, I am told, likewise wanted to leave the ship.

It was of no use for me to recount my attempts to bring back the offenders to a sense of their duty. All I could do was by speaking to them in general. Still it was to no purpose, for I was kept securely bound, and no one except the guard suffered to come near me.

To Mr Samuel, the clerk, I am indebted for securing my journals and commission, with some material ship papers. Without these I had nothing to certify what I had done, and my honour and character might have been suspected, without the proper documents. All this he did with great resolution, though guarded and strictly watched. He attempted to save the timekeeper, and a box with my surveys, drawings, and remarks, for fifteen years past.

It appeared to me that Christian was some time in doubt whether he should keep the carpenter, or his mates. He decided to go with the latter, and the carpenter was ordered into the boat. He was permitted, but not without some opposition, to take his tool-chest.

More quarrel took place among the mutinous crew all the time. I asked for arms, but they laughed at me, and said I was familiar with the people among whom I was going, and therefore did not want them. Four cutlasses, however, were thrown into the boat, after we were veered astern.

The officers and men being in the boat, they only waited for me, of which the master-at-arms informed Christian; who then said, 'Come, Captain Bligh, your officers and men are now in the boat, and you must go with them. If you attempt to make the least resistance, you will instantly be put to death.'

Without further delay, with a tribe of armed ruffians about me, I was forced over the side, when they untied my hands. Being in the boat, we were veered astern by a rope, a few pieces of pork were thrown to us, and some clothes, also the cutlasses I have already mentioned. It was then that the armourer and carpenters called out to me to remember that they had no hand in the transaction. After having undergone a great deal of ridicule, and been kept for some time to make sport for these unfeeling wretches, we were, eighteen of us, at length cast adrift in the open ocean.

In all twenty-five—and the most able of the ship's company remained on the *Bounty*.

Christian, the chief of the mutineers, is from a respectable family in the North of England. This was the third voyage he had made with me. As I found it necessary to keep my ship's company at three watches, I had given him an order to take charge of the third, his abilities being thoroughly equal to the task; and by this means the master and gunner were not at watch and watch.

Heywood is also from a respectable family in the North of England, and a young man of abilities as well as Christian. I had taken great pains to instruct them, having entertained hopes that, as professional men, they would have become an asset to their country.

Young was well recommended, and had the look of an able stout seaman; he, however, fell short of what his appearance promised. In the account on why he was sent home, it was described: Edward Young, midshipman, aged twenty-two years. Dark complexion and rather a bad look—strong made—had lost several of his fore teeth, and those that remain were all rotten.

Stewart was a young man of creditable parents in the Orkneys; at which place, on the return of the Resolution from the South Seas, in 1780, we received so many civilities that, on that account only, I should gladly have taken him with me: but, independent of this recommendation, he was a seaman, and had always borne a good character.

Notwithstanding the roughness with which I was treated, the remembrance of past kindness produced some signs of remorse in Christian. When they were forcing me out of the ship, I asked him if this treatment was a proper return for the many instances he had received from our friendship? He appeared disturbed at my question, and answered with much emotion, 'That—Captain Bligh—that is the thing—I am in hell—I am in hell!'

As soon as I had time to reflect, I felt an inward satisfaction, which prevented any depression of my spirits. A few hours before, my situation had been flattering. I had a ship in the most perfect order, and well stored with every necessary both for service and health.

It will very naturally be asked, what could be the reason for such a revolt? In answer to which I can only admit that the mutineers had flattered themselves with the hopes of a more happy life among the Otaheitans than they could possibly enjoy in England. The ship, indeed, while within our sight, steered to the west northwest but I considered this only as a joke; for when we were sent away —'Huzza for Otaheite!'—was frequently heard among the mutineers.

The women of Otaheite were pretty, mild and cheerful in their manners and conversation, possessed of great sensibility and had sufficient delicacy to make them admired and beloved. The chiefs were so much attached to the people, that they rather encouraged their stay among them than otherwise, and even made them promises of large possessions.

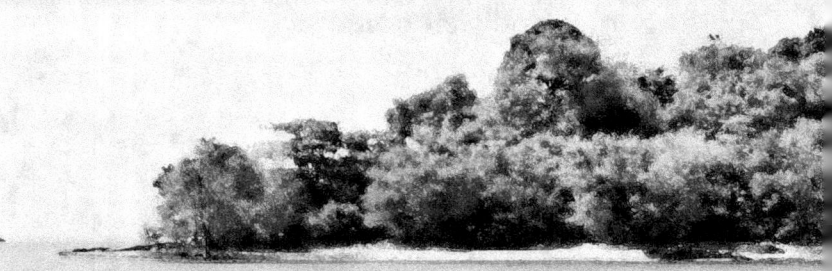

Under these and many other circumstances, it is now perhaps not so much to be wondered at, though scarcely possible to have been foreseen, that a set of sailors, most of them void of connections, should be led away. Especially they imagined it in their power to fix themselves in the midst of plenty, on one of the finest islands in the world. The utmost, however, that any commander could have supposed to have happened is, that some of the people would have been tempted to desert. But if it should be asserted that a commander is to guard against an act of mutiny and piracy in his own ship, more than by the common rules of service, it is as much as to say that he must sleep locked up, and when awake, be armed with pistols.

Desertions have happened, more or less, from most of the ships that have been at the Society Islands; but it has always been in the commander's power to make the chiefs return their people.

The secrecy of this mutiny was beyond all conception. Thirteen of the party, who were with me, had always lived forward among the seamen; yet neither they, nor the messmates of Christian, Stewart, Heywood and Young, had ever observed any circumstance that made them in the least suspect what was going on. To such a close-planned act of villainy, my mind being entirely free from any suspicion, it is not wonderful that I fell a sacrifice. Perhaps, if there had been marines on board, a sentinel at my cabin-door might have prevented it. I slept with the door always open, that the officer of the watch might have access to me on all occasions, not assuming any possibility of such a conspiracy. Had their mutiny been occasioned by any grievances, either real or imaginary, I must have discovered symptoms of their discontent. That would have put me on my guard; but the ease was far otherwise. Christian, in particular, I was on the most friendly terms with. That very day he was engaged to have dined with me; and the preceding night he excused himself from eating with me, on pretence of being unwell; for which I felt concerned, having no suspicions of his integrity and honour.

* * *

Such was the story published by Lieutenant Bligh immediately on his return to England, after one of the most distressing and perilous passages over nearly four thousand miles of the wide ocean, with others, in an open boat. The story obtained implicit credit; and though Lieutenant Bligh's character never stood high in the navy for suavity of manners or mildness of temper, he was always considered an excellent seaman.

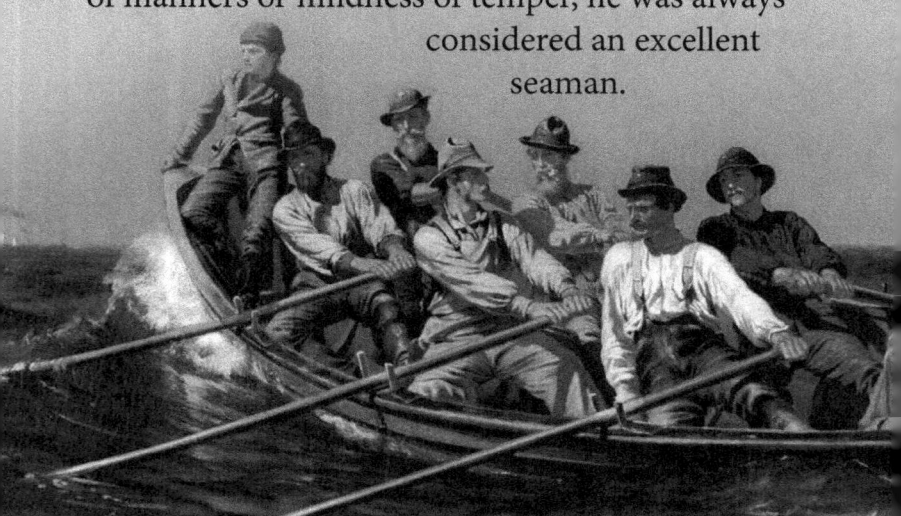

It was pretty evident, therefore, that the mutiny was not, as Bligh in his narrative stated it to have been, the result of a conspiracy. It would be seen by the minutes of the court-martial, that the whole affair was planned and executed between the hours of four and eight o'clock, on the morning of 28 April, when Christian had the watch upon deck.

The tide of public applause set as strongly in favour of Bligh, on account of his sufferings and the successful issue of his daring enterprise. Bligh was promoted by the Admiralty to the rank of Commander, and speedily sent out a second time to transport the breadfruit to the West Indies, which he successfully accomplished. His Majesty's government were no sooner informed about the atrocious act of piracy and mutiny than it determined to adopt every possible means to punish the perpetrators. For this purpose, the *Pandora* frigate, of twenty-four guns and one hundred and sixty men, was dispatched under the command of Captain Edward. They were given orders to proceed, in the first instance, to Otaheite

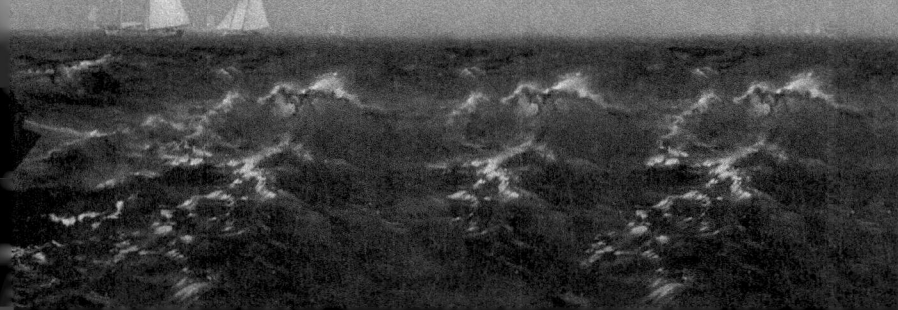

or Pitcairn Islands, and not finding the mutineers there, to visit the different groups of the Society and Friendly Islands, and others in the neighbouring parts of the Pacific, using his best efforts to seize and bring the mutineers back home in confinement.

The *Pandora* anchored in Matavai Bay on 23 March 1791. Captain Edward, in his narrative, stated: Joseph Coleman, the armourer of the *Bounty*, attempted to come on board before the *Pandora* had anchored. On reaching the ship, he began to make inquiries of him after the *Bounty* and her people, and he seemed to be ready to give him any information that was required. The next who came on board, just after the ship had anchored, were Mr Peter Heywood and Mr Stewart, before any boat had been sent on shore. They were brought down to his cabin, when, after some conversation, Heywood asked if Mr Hayward (midshipman of the *Bounty*, but now lieutenant of the *Pandora*) was on board, as he had heard that he was. Lieutenant Hayward, whom he sent for, treated Heywood with a sort of contemptuous look, and began to enter into conversation with him regarding the *Bounty*;

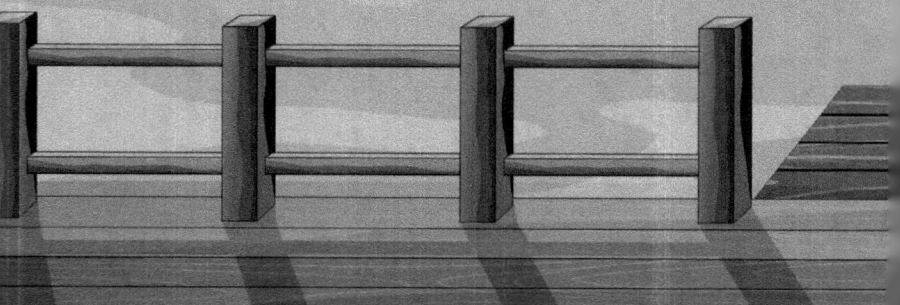

but Edward ordered him to desist, and called in the sentinel to take the prisoners into safe custody, and to put them in irons. Four other mutineers soon made their appearance; and from them and some of the natives, he learned that the rest of the *Bounty*'s people had built a schooner, with which they had sailed the day before from Matavai Bay to the northwest part of the island.

He goes on to say that, on this intelligence, he dispatched the two lieutenants, Corner and Hayward to intercept her. They soon got sight of her and chased her out to sea, but the schooner gained so much upon them, and night coming on, they were compelled to give up the pursuit and return to the ship.

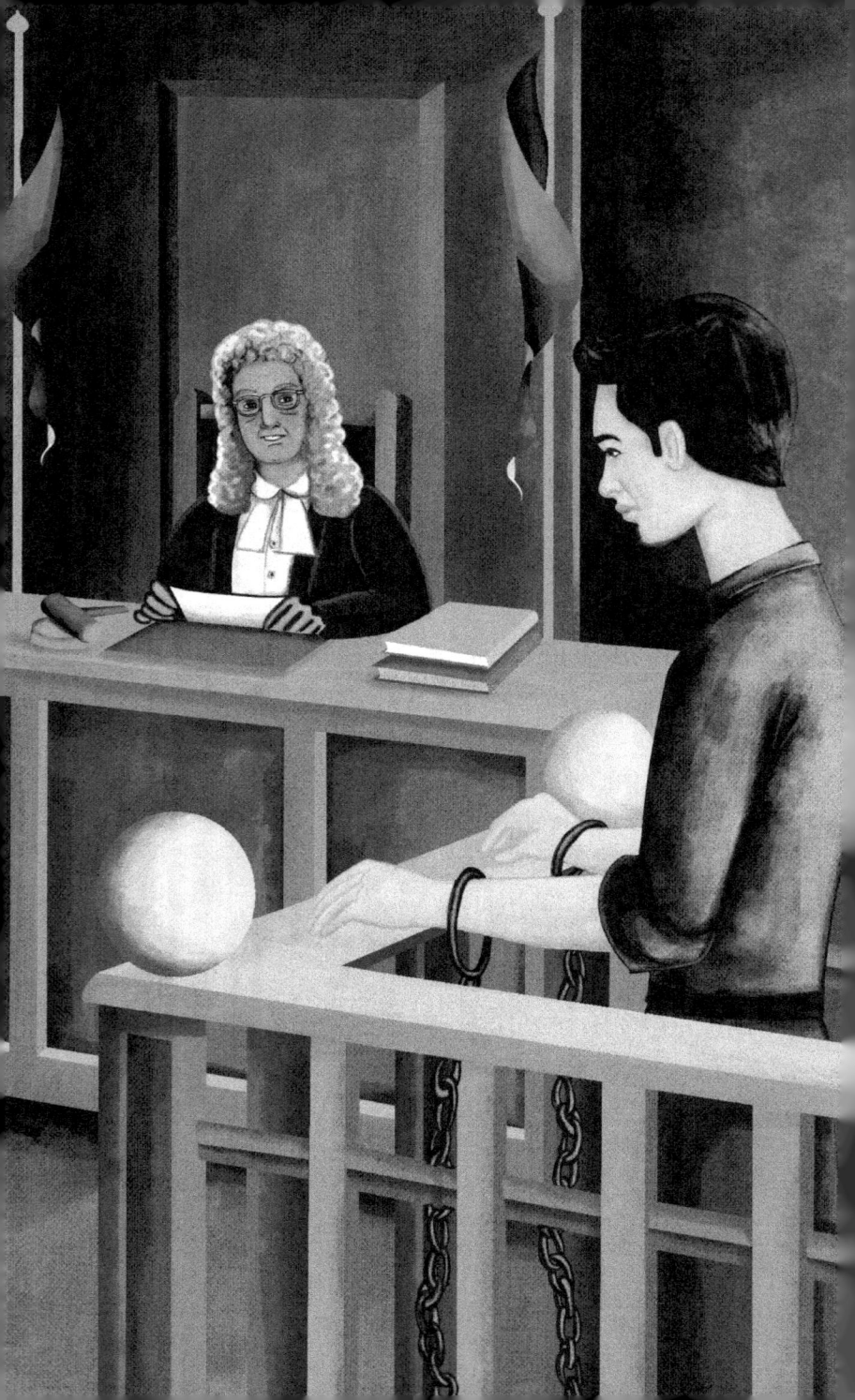

It was soon made known, however, that she had returned to Paparré, on which they were again despatched in search of her. Lieutenant Corner had taken three of the mutineers, and Hayward, on arriving at Paparré, found the schooner there, but the mutineers had abandoned her and fled to the mountains. He carried off the schooner, and returned the next day, when he learned they were not far off. The following morning, on hearing they were coming down, he drew up his party in order to receive them, and demanded them to lay down their arms and to go on one side, which they did.

Fourteen people were on board the *Pandora*. The other two, which made up the sixteen that had been left on the island, were murdered, as will appear presently.

Captain Edward put both legs of the two midshipmen in irons, and he branded them as 'piratical villains' and told that with the rest, being strongly handcuffed, should be put into a kind of round-house only eleven feet long, built as a prison, and aptly named 'Pandora's Box', which was entered by a scuttle in the roof, about eighteen inches square. This was done in order that they might be kept separate from the crew, and also to prevent them from having any communication with the natives. Captain Edward took every precaution to keep his prisoners in safe custody, and place them in confinement.

The Court assembled to try the prisoners on 12 September 1792. The charges set forth that Fletcher Christian, who was the mate of the *Bounty*, assisted by men, armed with muskets and bayonets, had violently and forcibly taken that ship from her commander, Lieutenant Bligh. That he, together with the master, boatswain, gunner and carpenter, and other persons, were forced into the launch and cast adrift—that Captain Edward, in the *Pandora*, was directed to proceed to Otaheite, and other islands in the South Seas, and to use his best endeavours to recover the said vessel.

Out of the mutineers imprisoned in the *Pandora*, Mr Peter Heywood, midshipman, was sentenced to death, but pardoned just before he was to be hung. So were six others out of sixteen in all, where three were killed and six were acquitted.

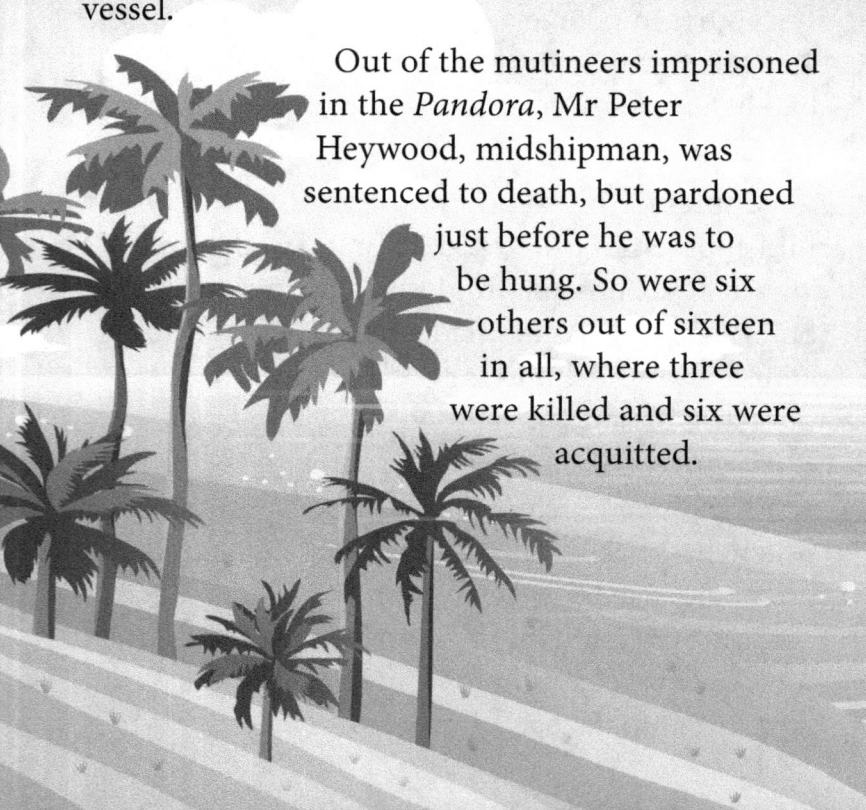

After the mutiny, Fletcher Christian, the acting lieutenant was murdered by the Otaheitans while he discovered Pitcairn Islands. Out of those, overall nine in number, who returned to Pitcairn Islands, none of them survived.

Many useful and salutary lessons of conduct could be drawn from this eventful history, more especially by officers of the navy, both old and young, as well as by those subordinate to them. The number of persons who remained in the *Bounty,* after her piratical seizure, and of course charged with the crime of mutiny, were twenty-five; that these subsequently separated into two parties, sixteen having landed at Otaheite, and afterwards taken from there in the *Pandora*, as prisoners, and nine having gone with the *Bounty* to Pitcairn's Island.

The conduct of Bligh, however mistaken he may have been in his mode of carrying on the duties of the ship, was the most exemplary throughout the long and dangerous voyage he performed in an open boat, on the wide ocean, with the most scanty supply of provisions and water, and in the worst weather.

The Adventures of Pinocchio

Carlo Collodi

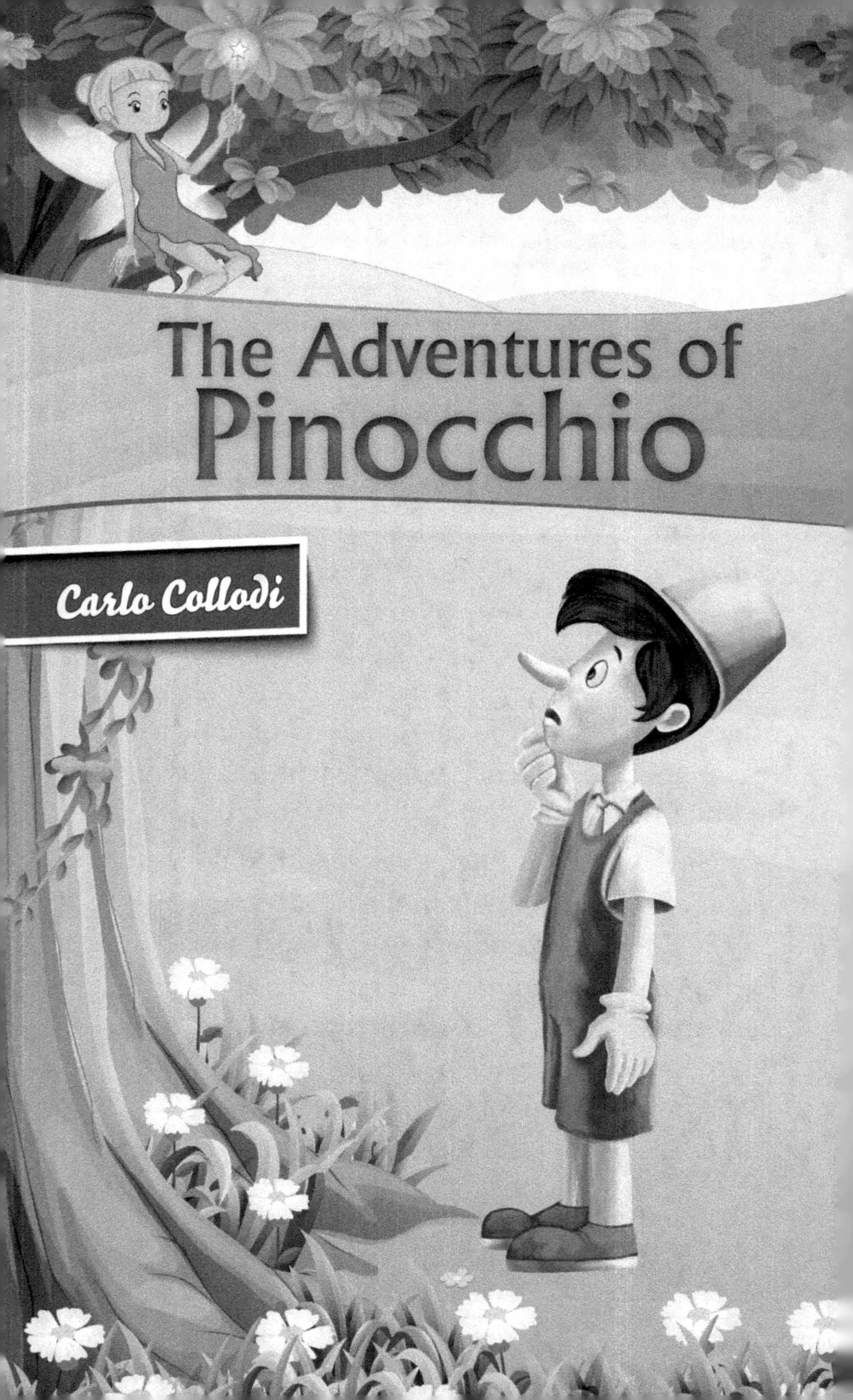

There was once upon a time a piece of wood in the shop of an old carpenter named Master Antonio. Everybody, however, called him Master Cherry because of the end of his nose, which was always as red and shiny as a ripe cherry.

No sooner had Master Cherry set eyes on the piece of wood than his face beamed with delight, and rubbing his hands together with satisfaction, he said softly to himself, 'This wood has come at the right moment; it will just do to make the leg of a little table.'

He immediately took a sharp axe with which he could remove the bark and the rough surface, but just as he was going to give the first stroke, he heard a very small voice, 'Do not strike me so hard!'

He turned his terrified eyes all around the room to try and discover where the little voice could possibly have come from, but he saw nobody! Who, then, could it be?

'I see how it is,' he said, laughing and scratching his wig, 'evidently that little voice was all my imagination. Let us set to work again.'

And, taking up the axe, he struck a tremendous blow on the piece of wood.

'Oh! Oh! You have hurt me!' cried the same little voice.

This time Master Cherry was stunned. As soon as he had recovered the use of his speech, he began to say, trembling with fear, 'But where on earth can that little voice have come from that said, "Oh! oh!?" Is it possible that this piece of wood can have learned to cry and to lament like a child? I cannot believe it. This piece of wood is nothing but a log for fuel like all the others, and thrown on the fire it would about suffice to boil a saucepan of beans. How then? Can anyone be hidden inside it? If anyone is hidden inside, so much the worse for him. I will settle him at once.'

So saying, he seized the poor piece of wood and commenced beating it without mercy against the walls of the room.

Then he stopped to listen if he could hear any little voice lamenting. He waited two minutes—nothing; five minutes—nothing; ten minutes—still nothing!

Putting the axe aside, he took his plane to polish the bit of wood; but whilst he was running it up and down he heard the same little voice say, laughing.

'Stop! you are tickling me all over!'

This time, poor Master Cherry fell down as if lightning had struck him. When he at last opened his eyes he found himself seated on the floor.

His face was changed, even the end of his nose, instead of being crimson, as it was nearly always, had become blue from fright.

At that moment someone knocked at the door.

'Come in,' said the carpenter, without having the strength to rise to his feet.

A lively little old man immediately walked into the shop. His name was Geppetto, but when the boys of the neighbourhood wished to make him angry, they called him Pudding, because his yellow wig greatly resembled a pudding made of Indian corn.

'Good day, Master Antonio,' said Geppetto; 'what are you doing there on the floor?'

'I am teaching the alphabet to the ants.'

'Much good may that do you.'

'What has brought you to me, neighbour Geppetto?'

'My legs. But to tell the truth, Master Antonio, I came to ask a favour from you.'

'Here I am, ready to serve you,' replied the carpenter, getting on his knees.

'This morning an idea came into my head.'

'Let us hear it.'

'I thought I would make a beautiful wooden puppet; one that could dance, fence, and leap like an acrobat. With this puppet, I would travel about the world to earn a piece of bread and a glass of wine. What do you think of it?'

'Bravo, Pudding!' exclaimed the same little voice, and it was impossible to say where it came from.

Hearing himself called Pudding, Geppetto became as red as a turkey cock from rage and, turning to the carpenter, he said in a fury,

'Why do you insult me?'

'Who insults you?'

'You called me Pudding!'

'It was not me!'

'Do you think I called myself Pudding? It was you, I say!'

'No!'

'Yes!'

'No!'

'Yes!'

And, becoming more and more angry, from words they came to blows, and, flying at each other's throats, they bit and fought, and scratched.

When the fight was over Master Antonio was in possession of Geppetto's yellow wig, and the latter discovered that the grey wig belonging to the carpenter remained between his teeth.

'Give me back my wig,' screamed Master Antonio.

'And you, return me mine, and let us be friends again.'

The two old men having each recovered his own wig, shook hands and swore that they would remain friends to the end of their lives.

'Well, then, neighbour Geppetto,' said the carpenter, to prove that peace was made, 'what is the favour that you wish from me?'

'I want a little wood to make my puppet; will you give me some?'

Master Antonio was delighted, and he immediately went to the bench and came back with the piece of wood that had caused him so much fear. But just as he was going to give it to his friend the piece of wood gave a shake and, twisting violently out of his hands, struck with all of its force against the dried-up shins of poor Geppetto.

'Ah! Is that the courteous way in which you make your presents, Master Antonio? You have almost lamed me!'

'I swear to you that it was not I!'

'Then you would have it that it was I?'

'The wood is entirely to blame!'

'I know that it was the wood; but it was you that hit my legs with it!'

'I did not hit you with it!'

'Liar!'

'Geppetto, don't insult me or I will call you Pudding!'

'Knave!'

'Pudding!'

'Donkey!'

'Pudding!'

'Baboon!'

'Pudding!'

On hearing himself called Pudding for the third time, Geppetto, mad with rage, fell upon the carpenter and they fought desperately.

When the battle was over, Master Antonio had two more scratches on his nose, and his opponent had lost two buttons off his waistcoat. Their accounts being thus squared, they shook hands and swore to remain good friends for the rest of their lives.

Geppetto carried off his fine piece of wood and, thanking Master Antonio, returned limping to his house.

Geppetto lived in a small ground-floor room that was only lighted from the staircase. The furniture could not have been simpler—a rickety chair, a poor bed and a broken-down table. At the end of the room, there was a fireplace with a lighted fire; but the fire was painted, and by the fire was a painted saucepan that was boiling and sending out a cloud of smoke that looked exactly like real smoke.

As soon as he reached home, Geppetto took his tools and set to work to cut out and model his puppet.

'What name shall I give him?' he said to himself; 'I think I will call him Pinocchio. It is a name that will bring him luck. I once knew a whole family so called. There was Pinocchio the father, Pinocchia the mother, and Pinocchi the children, and all of them did well. The richest of them was a beggar.'

Having found a name for his puppet Geppetto began to work in earnest, and he first made his hair, then his forehead, and then his eyes.

The eyes being finished, imagine his astonishment when he perceived that they moved and looked fixedly at him.

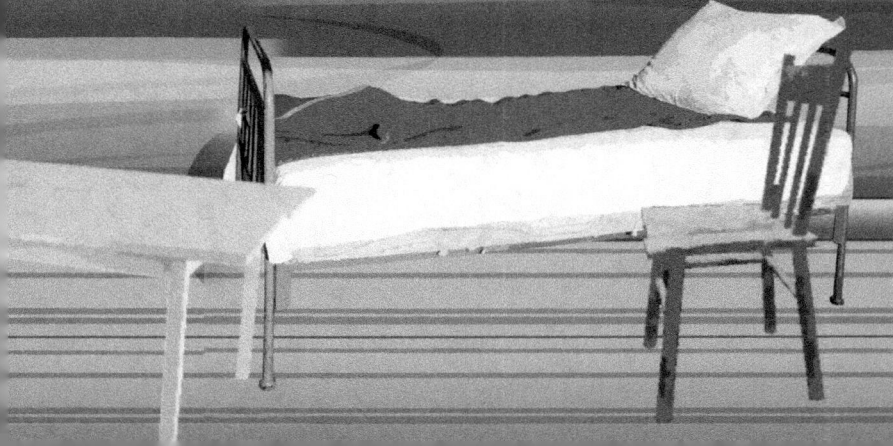

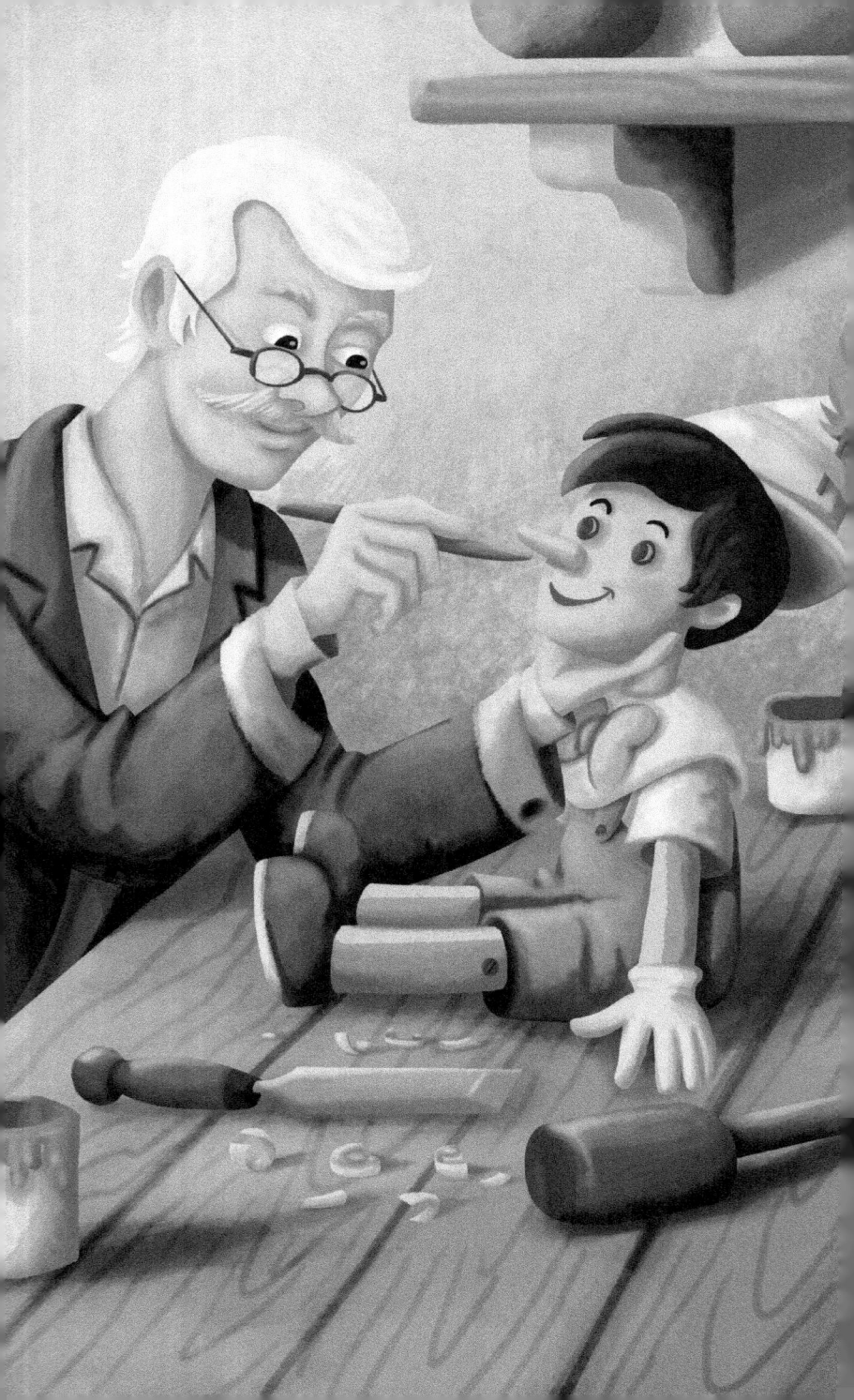

Geppetto, seeing himself stared at by those two wooden eyes, said in an angry voice,

'Wicked wooden eyes, why do you look at me?'

No one answered.

He then proceeded to carve the nose, but no sooner had he made it than it began to grow. And it grew, and grew, and grew, until in a few minutes it had become an immense nose that seemed as if it would never end.

Poor Geppetto tired himself out with cutting it off, but the more he cut and shortened it, the longer did that nose become!

The mouth was not even completed when it began to laugh and deride him.

'Stop laughing!' said Geppetto, provoked; but he might as well have spoken to the wall.

'Stop laughing, I say!' he roared in a threatening tone.

The mouth then ceased laughing, but put out its tongue as far as it would go.

Geppetto, not to spoil his handiwork, pretended not to see and continued his work. After the mouth he fashioned the chin, then the throat, then the shoulders, the stomach, the arms and the hands.

The hands were scarcely finished when Geppetto felt his wig snatched from his head. He turned round, and what did he see? He saw his yellow wig in the puppet's hand.

'Pinocchio! Give me back my wig instantly!'

But Pinocchio, instead of returning it, put it on his own head.

Geppetto felt sadder and more melancholy than he had ever been in his life before; and, turning to Pinocchio, he said to him.

'You, young rascal! You are not yet completed and you are already beginning to show disrespect to your father! That is bad, my boy, very bad!'

And he dried his tear.

The legs and the feet remained to be done.

When Geppetto had finished the feet he received a slap on his nose.

'I deserve it!' he said to himself. 'I should have thought of it sooner! Now it is too late!'

He then took the puppet under the arms and placed him on the floor to teach him to walk.

Pinocchio's legs were stiff and he could not move, but Geppetto led him by the hand and showed him how to put one foot before the other.

When his legs became limber, Pinocchio began to walk by himself and to run about the room, until, having gone out of the house door, he jumped into the street and escaped.

Poor Geppetto rushed after him but was not able to overtake him, for that rascal Pinocchio leaped in front of him like a hare and knocking his wooden feet together against the pavement made as much clatter as twenty pairs of peasants' clogs.

'Stop him! Stop him!' shouted Geppetto; but the people in the street, seeing a wooden puppet running like a racehorse, stood still in astonishment to look at it, and laughed and laughed.

At last, as good luck would have it, a soldier arrived who, hearing the uproar, imagined that a colt had escaped from his master. Planting himself courageously with his legs apart in the middle of the road, he waited with the determined purpose of stopping him and thus preventing the chance of worse disasters.

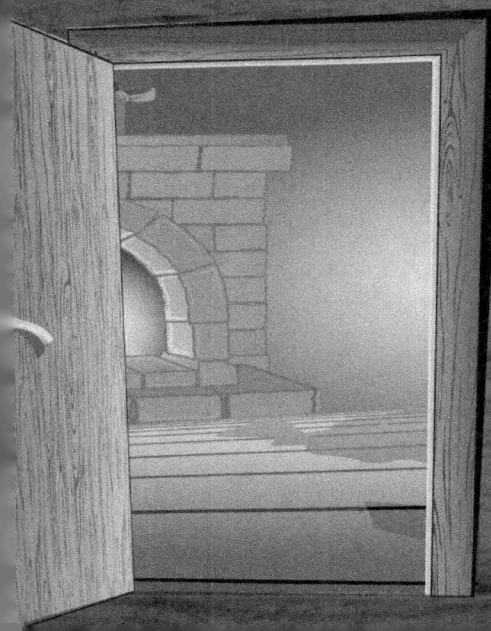

The soldier without disturbing himself in the least caught Pinocchio cleverly by the nose and gave him to Geppetto. Wishing to punish him, Geppetto intended to pull his ears at once. But imagine his feelings when he could not succeed in finding them. And do you know the reason? In his hurry to model him Geppetto had forgotten to make any ears.

Pinocchio threw himself on the ground and refused to take another step. One person after another gathered around the two. People commented on how Geppetto would go home and beat the puppet. It ended in so much being said and done that the soldier at last set Pinocchio at liberty and led Geppetto to prison. The poor man, not being ready with words to defend himself, cried like a calf and as he was being led away to prison sobbed out.

'Wretched boy! And to think how I laboured to make him a well-conducted puppet! But it serves me right! I should have thought of it sooner!'

One day, Pinocchio told Geppetto that to reward him for his kindness he will go to school.

'Good boy,' said Gepetto.

'But to go to school I shall want some clothes.'

Geppetto, who was poor and who did not have so much as a penny in his pocket, then made him a little dress of flowered paper, a pair of shoes from the bark of a tree, and a cap of the crumb of bread.

Pinocchio ran immediately to look at himself in a jar of water, and he was so pleased with his appearance that he said, strutting about like a peacock, 'I look quite like a gentleman!'

'Yes, indeed,' answered Geppetto, 'for bear in mind that it is not fine clothes that make the gentleman, but rather clean clothes.'

'By the by,' added the puppet, 'to go to school I am still in want—indeed, I am without the best thing, and the most important.'

'And what is it?'

'I have no spelling-book.'

'You are right: but what shall we do to get one?'

'It is quite easy. We have only to go to the bookseller's and buy it.'

'And the money?'

'I have got none.'

'Neither have I,' added the good old man, very sadly.

And Pinocchio, although he was a very merry boy, became sad also, because poverty, when it is real poverty, is understood by everybody—even by boys.

'Well, patience!' exclaimed Geppetto, all at once rising to his feet, and putting on his old coat, all patched and darned, he ran out of the house.

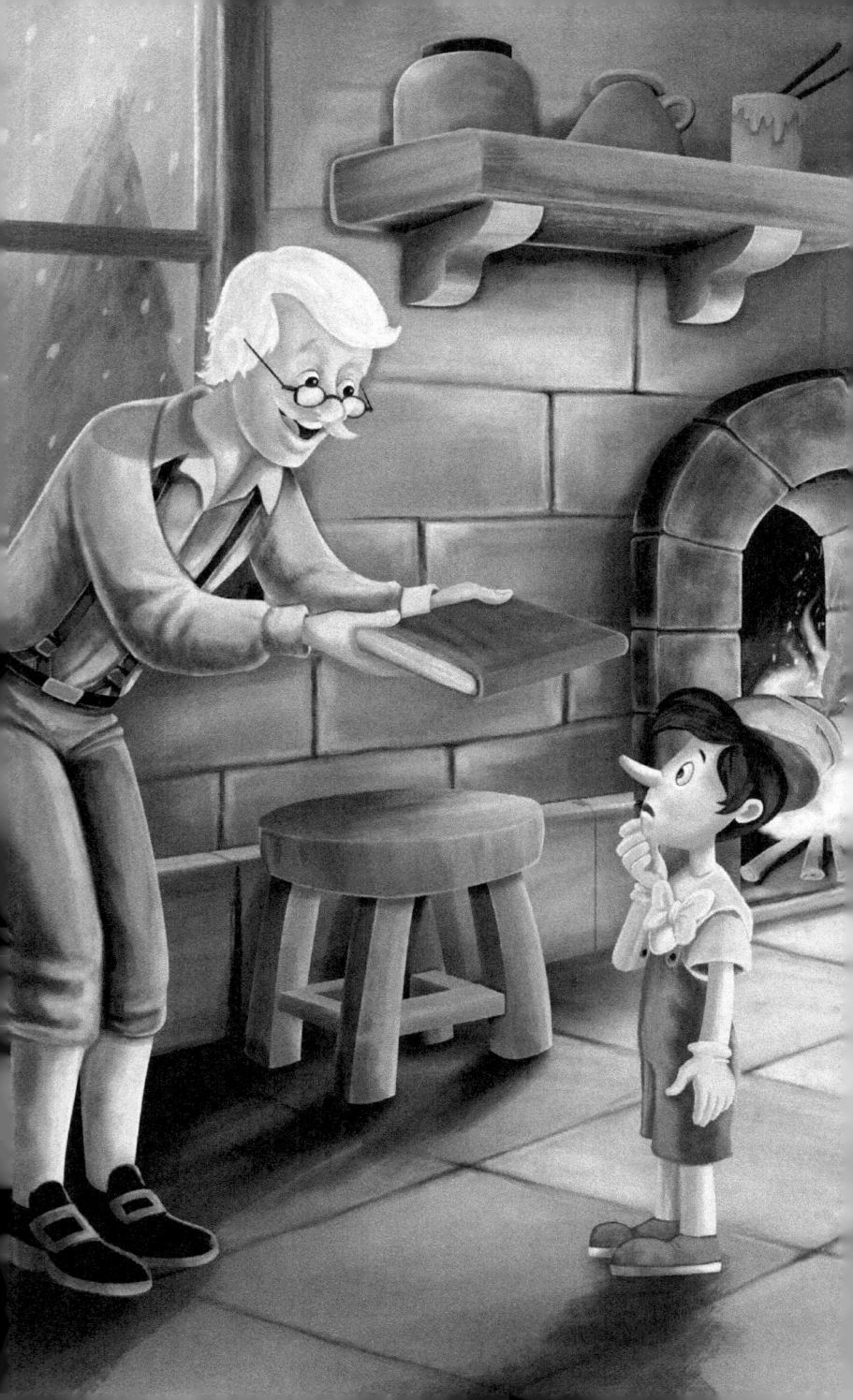

He returned shortly, holding in his hand a spelling-book for Pinocchio, but the old coat was gone. The poor man was in his shirt sleeves and outside it was snowing.

'And the coat, Papa?'

'I have sold it.'

'Why did you sell it?'

'Because I found it too hot.'

Pinocchio understood this answer in an instant, and unable to restrain the impulse of his good heart he sprang up and, throwing his arms around Geppetto's neck, he began kissing him repeatedly.

As soon as it stopped snowing Pinocchio set out for school with his fine spelling-book under his arm. As he went along, he began to imagine a thousand things in his little brain and to build a thousand castles in the air, one more beautiful than the other.

And, talking to himself, he said,

'Today at school I will learn to read at once; then tomorrow I will begin to write, and the day after tomorrow to draw. Then, with my acquirements, I will earn a great deal of money, and with the first money I have in my pocket I will immediately buy for my papa a beautiful new coat. But what am I saying? Cloth, indeed! It shall be all made of gold and silver, and it shall have diamond buttons. That poor man really deserves it, for to buy me books and have me taught he has remained in his shirt sleeves. And in this cold! It is only fathers who are capable of such sacrifices!'

Whilst he was saying this with great emotion, he thought that he heard music in the distance that sounded like fifes and the beating of a big drum: Fi-fie-fi, fi-fi-fi; zum, zum, zum.

He stopped and listened. The sounds came from the end of a cross street that led to a little village on the seashore.

'What can that music be? What a pity that I have to go to school, or else—'

And he remained uncertain. It was, however, necessary to come to a decision. Should he go to school? Or should he go after the fifes?

'Today I will go and hear the fifes, and tomorrow I will go to school,' finally decided the little devil, shrugging his shoulders.

The more he ran the nearer he heard the sounds of the fifes and the beating of the big drum: Fi-fi-fi; zum, zum, zum, zum.

At last, he found himself in the middle of a square quite full of people, who were all crowded around a building made of wood and canvas, and painted in a thousand colours.

'What is that building?' asked Pinocchio, turning to a little boy who belonged to the place.

'Read the placard—it is all written—and then you will know.'

'I would read it willingly, but it so happens that today I don't know how to read.'

'Bravo, blockhead! Then I will read it to you. The writing in red on that placard read as:

'THE GREAT PUPPET THEATRE.'

'Has the play begun long?'

'It is beginning now.'

'How much does it cost to go in?'

'A dime.'

Pinocchio, who was in a fever of curiosity, lost all control of himself, and without any shame he said to the little boy to whom he was talking:

'Would you lend me a dime until tomorrow?'

'I would lend it to you willingly,' said the other, 'but it so happens that today I cannot give it to you.'

'I will sell you my jacket for a dime,' the puppet then said to him.

'What do you think that I could do with a jacket of flowered paper? If there were rain and it got wet, it would be impossible to get it off my back.'

'Will you buy my shoes?'

'They would only be of use to light the fire.'

'How much will you give me for my cap?'

'That would be wonderful indeed! A cap of breadcrumb! There would be a risk of the mice coming to eat it whilst it is on my head.'

Pinocchio was on thorns. He was on the point of making another offer, but he had not the courage. He hesitated, uncertain and remorseful. At last he said,

'Will you give me a dime for this new spelling-book?'

'I am a boy and I don't buy from boys,' replied his little speaker, who had much more sense than he had.

'I will buy the spelling-book for a dime,' called out a hawker of old clothes, who had been listening to the conversation.

And the book was sold there and then. And to think that poor Geppetto had remained at home trembling with cold in his shirt sleeves in order that his son should have a spelling-book.

When Pinocchio came into the little puppet theatre, an incident occurred that almost produced a revolution.

The curtain had gone up and the play had already begun.

On the stage Harlequin and Punch were as usual quarrelling with each other and threatening every moment to come to blows.

All at once Harlequin stopped short and, turning to the public, he pointed with his hand to someone far down in the pit and exclaimed in a dramatic tone,

'Gods of the heavens! Do I dream or am I awake? But surely that is Pinocchio!'

'It is indeed Pinocchio!' cried Punch.

'It is indeed himself!' said Miss Rose, peeping from behind the scenes.

'It is Pinocchio! It is Pinocchio!' shouted all the puppets in chorus, leaping from all sides on to the stage. 'It is Pinocchio! It is our brother Pinocchio! Long live Pinocchio!'

'Pinocchio, come up here to me,' cried Harlequin, 'and throw yourself into the arms of your wooden brothers!'

At this affectionate invitation Pinocchio made a leap from the end of the pit into the reserved seats; another leap landed him on the head of the leader of the orchestra, and he then sprang upon the stage.

At that moment out came the showman.

'Why have you come to raise a disturbance in my theatre?'

'Believe me, honoured sir, it was not my fault!'

'That is enough! Tonight we will settle our accounts.'

As soon as the play was over the showman went into the kitchen, where a fine sheep, preparing for his supper, was turning slowly on the spit in front of the fire. As there was not enough wood to finish roasting and browning it, he called Harlequin and Punch, and said to them,

'Bring that puppet here: you will find him hanging on a nail. It seems to me that he is made of very dry wood and I am sure that if he were thrown on the fire he would make a beautiful blaze for the roast.'

At first Harlequin and Punch hesitated; but, appalled by a severe glance from their master, they obeyed. In a short time they returned to the kitchen carrying poor Pinocchio, who was wriggling like an eel taken out of water and screaming desperately, 'Papa! Papa! Save me! I will not die, I will not die!'

'Thank you! And your papa and your mamma, are they still alive?' asked Fire-Eater.

'Papa, yes; my mamma I have never known.'

'Who can say what a sorrow it would be for your poor old father if I were to have you thrown amongst those burning coals?! Poor old man! I pity him! Etchoo! Etchoo! Etchoo!' and he sneezed again three times.

'Bless you,' said Pinocchio.

'Thank you! All the same, some compassion is due to me, for as you see I have no more wood with which to finish roasting my mutton, and, to tell you the truth, under the circumstances you would have been of great use to me! However, I have had pity on you, so I must have patience. Instead of you, I will burn under the spit one of the puppets belonging to my company. Ho there, policemen!'

At this call two wooden policemen immediately appeared. They were very long and very thin, and had on cocked hats, and held unsheathed swords in their hands.

The showman said to them in a hoarse voice,

'Take Harlequin, bind him securely, and then throw him on the fire to burn. I am determined that my mutton shall be well roasted.'

Only imagine that poor Harlequin! His terror was so great that his legs bent under him, and he fell with his face on the ground.

At this agonizing sight Pinocchio, weeping bitterly, threw himself at the showman's feet and, bathing his long beard with his tears, he began to say, in a humble voice,

'Have pity, Sir Fire-Eater!'

'Here there are no sirs,' the showman answered severely.

'Have pity, Sir Knight!'

'Here there are no knights!'

'Have pity, Commander!'

'Here there are no commanders!'

'Have pity, Excellence!'

Upon hearing himself called Excellence the showman began to smile and became at once kinder and more friendly. Turning to Pinocchio, he asked,

'Well, what do you want from me?'

'I request you to pardon poor Harlequin.'

'For him there can be no pardon. As I have spared you he must be put on the fire, for I am determined that my mutton shall be well roasted.'

'In that case,' cried Pinocchio proudly, rising and throwing away his cap of breadcrumb—'in that case I know my duty. Come on, policemen! Bind me and throw me amongst the flames. No, it is not just that poor Harlequin, my true friend, should die for me!'

These words, pronounced in a loud, heroic voice, made all the puppets who were present cry. Even the policemen, although they were made of wood, wept like two newly born lambs.

Fire-Eater at first remained as hard and unmoved as ice, but little by little he began to melt and to sneeze. And, having sneezed four or five times, he opened his arms affectionately and said to Pinocchio,

'You are a good, brave boy! Come here and give me a kiss.'

Pinocchio ran at once and, climbing like a squirrel up the showman's beard, he deposited a hearty kiss on the point of his nose.

'Then the pardon is granted?' asked poor Harlequin in a faint voice that was scarcely audible.

'The pardon is granted!' answered Fire-Eater; he then added, sighing and shaking his head,

'I must have patience! Tonight I shall have to resign myself to eat the mutton half raw; but another time, woe to him who displeases me!'

At the news of the pardon, the puppets all ran to the stage and, having lighted the lamps and chandeliers as if for a full-dress performance, they began to leap and to dance merrily. At dawn they were still dancing.

The following day Fire-Eater called Pinocchio to one side and asked him,

'What is your father's name?'

'Geppetto.'

'And what trade does he follow?'

'He is a beggar.'

'Does he gain much?'

'Gain much? Why, he has never a penny in his pocket. Only think, in order to buy a spelling-book so that I could go to school he was obliged to sell the only coat he had to wear—a coat that, between patches and darns, was not fit to be seen.'

'Poor devil! I feel so sorry for him! Here are five gold pieces. Go at once and take them to him with my compliments.'

Pinocchio was overjoyed and thanked the showman a thousand times. He embraced all the puppets of the company one by one, even the policemen, and set out to return home.

But he had not gone far when he met on the road a Fox lame of one foot, and a Cat blind of both eyes, and they were going along helping each other like good companions in misfortune. The Fox, who was lame, walked leaning on the Cat; and the Cat, who was blind, was guided by the Fox.

They warmly greeted Pinocchio and told him that they knew his father well, and that they last saw him shiver in the cold. While Pinocchio felt sad about his father's condition, they used this situation to their advantage to ask him what he would do of all that money.

'First of all,' answered the puppet, 'I intend to buy a new coat for my papa, made of gold and silver, and with diamond buttons; and then I will buy a spelling-book for myself.'

'For yourself?'

'Yes indeed, for I wish to go to school to study in earnest.'

'Would you like to make out of your five miserable sovereigns, a hundred, a thousand, two thousand?'

'I should think so! But in what way?'

'The way is easy enough. Instead of returning home you must go with us.'

'And where do you wish to take me?'

'To the land of the Owls.'

'Between today and tomorrow your five sovereigns would have become two thousand.'

'Two thousand!' said the Cat.

'But how is it possible that they could become so many?' asked Pinocchio, remaining with his mouth open from astonishment.

'I will explain it to you at once,' said the Fox. 'You must know that in the land of the Owls there is a sacred field called by everybody the Field of Miracles. In this field, you must dig a little hole, and you put into it, we will say, one gold sovereign. You then cover up the hole with a little earth; you must water it with two pails of water from the fountain, then, sprinkle it with two pinches of salt, and when night comes you can go quietly to bed. In the meanwhile, during the night, the gold piece will grow and flower, and in the morning when you get up and return to the field, what do you find? You find a beautiful tree laden with as many gold sovereigns as a fine ear of corn has grains in the month of June.'

'What good people!' thought Pinocchio to himself, and, forgetting there and then his papa, the new coat, the spelling-book, and all his good resolutions, he said to the Fox and the Cat,

'Let us be off at once. I will go with you.'

They walked and walked and walked. At last, towards evening, dead tired, they came to the Inn of the Red Lobster.

'Let us stop here a while,' said the Fox, 'to eat a bite and rest for a few hours. At midnight we'll start out again, for at dawn tomorrow we must be at the Field of Wonders.'

They went into the Inn and all three sat down at the same table. However, none of them were very hungry.

At midnight, the Fox and the Cat tricked Pinocchio and hanged him to a branch of an oak tree.

They left him hanging, and he was refusing to part with his money. If poor Pinocchio had dangled there much longer, all hope would have been lost. Luckily for him, a Fairy noticed him hanging and sent for rescue. Pinocchio was finally tucked into a bed in her house.

'If you have lost gold pieces in the wood near here,' said the Fairy, 'we will look for them and we shall find them: because everything that is lost in that wood is always found.'

'Ah! Now I remember all about it,' replied the puppet, getting quite confused. 'I didn't lose the four gold pieces, I swallowed them whilst I was drinking your medicine.'

At this lie his nose grew to such an extraordinary length that poor Pinocchio could not move in any direction. If he turned to one side, he struck his nose against the bed or the window-panes, if he turned to the other he struck it against the walls or the door, if he raised his head a little he ran the risk of sticking it into one of the Fairy's eyes.

And the Fairy looked at him and laughed.

'What are you laughing at?' asked the puppet, very confused and anxious at finding his nose growing so prodigiously.

'I am laughing at the lie you have told.'

'And how can you possibly know that I have told a lie?'

'Lies, my dear boy, are found out immediately, because they are of two sorts. There are lies that have short legs, and lies that have long noses. Your lie, as it happens, is one of those that have a long nose.'

Pinocchio, not knowing where to hide himself for shame, tried to run out of the room; but he did not succeed, for his nose had increased so much that it could no longer pass through the door.

Once when Pinocchio had gone way ahead swimming into the sea, he saw in the midst of the sea a rock that seemed to be made of white marble, and on the summit, there stood a beautiful little goat, which bleated lovingly and made signs to him to approach.

But the most exceptional thing was this. The little goat's hair, instead of being white or black, or a mixture of two colours as is usual with other goats, was blue, and a very vivid blue, greatly resembling the hair of the beautiful Child.

He swam with redoubled strength and energy towards the white rock; and he was already half-way there when he saw, rising up out of the water and coming to meet him, the horrible head of a sea monster. His wide-open, cavernous mouth and his three rows of enormous teeth would have been terrifying to look at even in a picture.

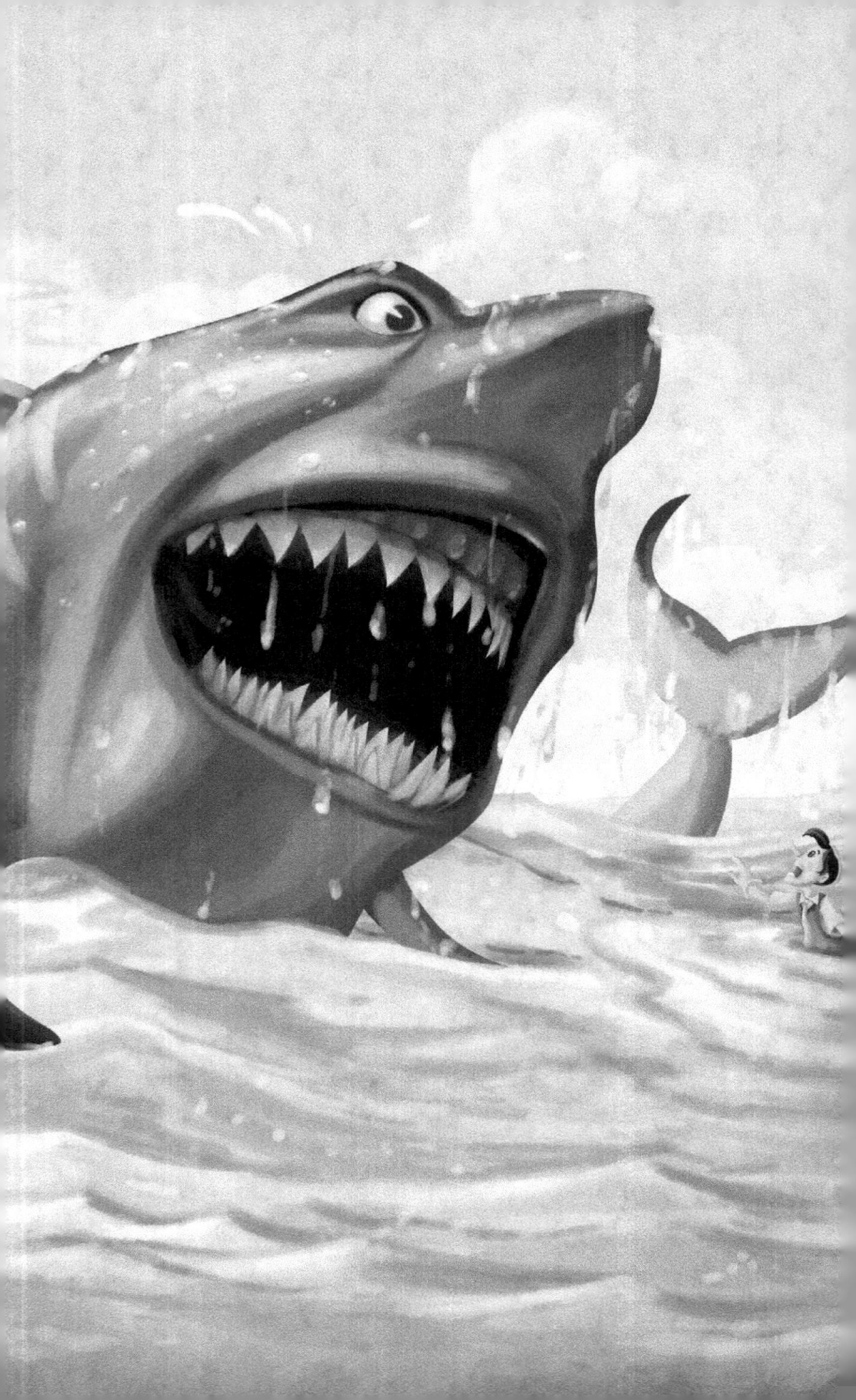

It was a dogfish shark and he couldn't escape from being swallowed in it. Pinocchio began to grope his way in the dark through the body of the shark, taking a step at a time in the direction of the light that he saw shining dimly at a great distance. Later, he found it was his father.

He wanted to laugh, he wanted to cry, he wanted to say a thousand things, and instead he could only stammer out a few confused and broken words. At last, he succeeded in uttering a cry of joy, and, opening his arms, he threw them around the little old man's neck, and began to shout,

'Oh, my dear Papa! I have found you at last! I will never leave you more, never more, never more!'

'Then my eyes tell me true?' said the little old man, rubbing his eyes, 'then you are really my dear Pinocchio?'

'Yes, yes, I am Pinocchio, really Pinocchio! And you have quite forgiven me, have you not? Oh, my dear Papa, how good you are! And to think that I, on the contrary—Oh! but if you only knew what misfortunes have been poured on my head, and all that has befallen me!'

And they walked for some time and traversed the body and the stomach of the shark. But when they had arrived at the point where the monster's big throat began, they thought it better to stop to give a good look around and to choose the best moment for escaping.

The shark, being very old, and suffering from asthma and palpitation of the heart, was obliged to sleep with his mouth open. Pinocchio, therefore, having approached the entrance to his throat, and, looking up, could see beyond the enormous gaping mouth a large piece of starry sky and beautiful moonlight.

'This is the moment to escape,' he said, turning to his father, 'the shark is sleeping like a dormouse, the sea is calm, and it is as light as day. Follow me, dear Papa, and in a short time we shall be in safety.'

They immediately climbed up the throat of the sea-monster, and, having reached his immense mouth, they began to walk on tiptoe down his tongue.

Before taking the final leap, the puppet said to his father,

'Get on my shoulders and put your arms tightly around my neck. I will take care of the rest.'

They finally happily escaped to living a new life.

Soon after, one night, while Pinocchio slept he thought that he saw the Fairy, smiling and beautiful, who, after having kissed him, said to him,

'Well done, Pinocchio! To reward you for your good heart I will forgive you for all that is past. Boys, who minister tenderly to their parents and assist them in their misery and weaknesses, are deserving of great praise and affection, even if they cannot be cited as examples of obedience and good behaviour. Try and do better in the future and you will be happy.'

At this moment his dream ended and Pinocchio opened his eyes and awoke.

But imagine his astonishment when upon awakening he discovered that he was no longer a wooden puppet, but that he had become instead a boy, like all other boys. He gave a glance round and saw that the straw walls of the hut had disappeared, and that he was in a pretty little room furnished and arranged with a simplicity that was almost elegant. Jumping out of bed he found a new suit of clothes ready for him, a new cap and a pair of new boots that fitted him beautifully.

'How ridiculous I was when I was a puppet! And how glad I am that I have become a well-behaved little boy!'

King Solomon's Mines

H. Rider Haggard

It was eighteen months or so ago since first I met Sir Henry Curtis and Captain Good while sailing to Natal from Cape Town.

They were among the passengers who excited my curiosity. One, a gentleman of about thirty, was perhaps the biggest-chested and longest-armed man I ever saw. I discovered afterwards that Sir Henry Curtis, for that was the big man's name, is of Danish blood. He also reminded me strongly of somebody else, but at the time, I could not remember who it was.

The other man, who stood talking to Sir Henry, was stout and dark, and of quite a different cut. He was Captain John Good, a naval officer, a lieutenant of thirty-one. After seventeen years of service, he had been turned out of Her Majesty's employ with the honour of a commander's rank.

In some time I heard his voice, 'That pendulum's wrong; it is not properly weighted.'

'Indeed, now what makes you think so?' I asked.

'Think so. I don't think at all. Why there'—as she righted herself after a roll—'if the ship had really rolled to the degree that thing pointed to, then she would never have rolled again, that's all. But it is just like these merchant skippers, they are always so careless.'

Just then the dinner-bell rang, and I was not sorry, for it is a dreadful thing to have to listen to an officer of the Royal Navy when he gets on to that subject. I only knew one worse thing, and that was to hear a merchant skipper express his opinion of officers of the Royal Navy.

Captain Good and I went down to dinner together, and there we found Sir Henry Curtis already seated. He and Captain Good were seated together, and I sat opposite to them. The captain and I soon fell into talk about shooting and what not; he asked me many questions, for he was very inquisitive about all sorts of things, and I answered them as well as I could. Presently he got on to elephants.

'Ah, sir,' called out somebody who was sitting near me, 'you've reached the right man for that; Hunter Quatermain should be able to tell you about elephants if anybody can.'

Sir Henry, who had been sitting quiet listening to our talk, started visibly.

'Excuse me, sir, but is your name Allan Quatermain?' he asked.

I said that it was.

The big man made no further remark, but I heard him mutter 'fortunate' into his beard.

Before long, dinner ended, and as we were leaving the saloon, Sir Henry strolled up and asked me if I would come into his cabin to smoke a pipe. I accepted, and he led the way to the Dunkeld deck cabin. Sir Henry sent the steward for a bottle of whisky, and the three of us sat down and lit our pipes.

'Mr Quatermain,' said Sir Henry Curtis, when the man had brought the whisky and lit the lamp, 'the year before last about this time, you were, I believe, at a place called Bamangwato, to the north of the Transvaal.'

'I was,' I answered, rather surprised that this gentleman should be so well acquainted with my movements, which were not, so far as I was aware, considered of general interest.

'You were trading there, were you not?' put in Captain Good, in his quick way.

'I was. I took up a wagon-load of goods, made a camp outside the settlement, and stopped till I had sold them.'

'Did you happen to meet a man called Neville there?'

'Oh, yes; he outspanned alongwith me for a fortnight to rest his oxen before going on to the interior. I had a letter from a lawyer a few months back, asking me if I knew what had become of him, which I answered to the best of my ability at the time.'

'Yes,' said Sir Henry, 'your letter was forwarded to me. You said in it that the gentleman called Neville left Bamangwato at the beginning of May in a wagon with a driver.'

'Yes.'

Then came a pause.

'Mr Quatermain,' said Sir Henry suddenly, 'I suppose you know or can guess nothing more of the reasons of my—of Mr Neville's journey to the northwards, or as to what point that journey was directed?'

'I heard something,' I answered, and stopped. The subject was one that I did not care to discuss.

Sir Henry and Captain Good looked at each other, and Captain Good nodded.

'Mr Quatermain,' said Sir Henry, 'I am going to tell you a story, and ask your advice.'

I bowed and drank some whisky and water to hide my confusion, for I am a modest man—and Sir Henry went on.

'Mr Neville was my brother.'

'Oh,' I said, starting, for now I knew of whom Sir Henry had reminded me when first I saw him.

'He was,' went on Sir Henry, 'my only and younger brother, and till five years ago I do not suppose that we were ever a month away from each other. But just about five years ago a misfortune befell us, as sometimes does happen in families. We quarrelled bitterly, and I behaved unjustly to my brother in my anger.'

'As I daresay you know,' went on Sir Henry, 'if a man dies without leaving behind a legal will, and has no property but land, it all descends to his eldest son. It so happened that just at the time when we quarrelled our father died. He had put off making his will until it was too late.

The result was that my brother, who had not been brought up to any profession, was left without a penny. Of course, it would have been my duty to provide for him, but at the time the quarrel between us was so bitter that I did not offer to do anything. It was not that I grudged him justice, but I waited for him. I am sorry to trouble you with all this, Mr Quatermain, but I must make things clear?'

'Of course,' said I, for I rather pride myself on my discretion, for which, as Sir Henry had heard, I have some repute.

'Well,' went on Sir Henry, 'my brother had a few hundred pounds to his account at the time. Without saying anything to me he drew out this sum, and, having adopted the name of Neville, started off for South Africa in the wild hope of making a fortune. This I learned afterwards. Some three years passed, and I heard nothing of my brother, though I wrote several times. I'm sure the letters never reached him. But as time went on I grew more and more troubled about him. I found out, Mr Quatermain, that blood is thicker than water.'

'That's true,' I said, thinking of my boy Harry.

'I found out, Mr Quatermain, that I would have given half my fortune to know that my brother George, the only relation I possess, was safe and well, and that I should see him again.'

'But you never did, Curtis,' said Captain Good, glancing at the big man's face.

'Well, Mr Quatermain, as time went on I became more and more anxious to find out if my brother was alive or dead, and if alive to get him home again. I set enquiries on foot, and your letter was one of the results. As far as it went it was satisfactory, for it showed that till lately George was alive, but it did not go far enough. So, to cut a long story short, I made up my mind to come out and look for him myself, and Captain Good was so kind as to come with me.'

'Yes,' said the captain, 'nothing else to do, you see. Turned out by my Lords of the Admiralty to starve on half pay... And now perhaps, sir, you will tell us what you know or have heard of the gentleman called Neville.'

'What was it that you heard about my brother's journey at Bamangwato?' asked Sir Henry, as I paused to fill my pipe before replying to Captain Good.

'I heard this,' I answered, 'and I have never mentioned it to a soul till today. I heard that he was starting for Solomon's Mines.'

'Solomon's Mines? Where are they?'

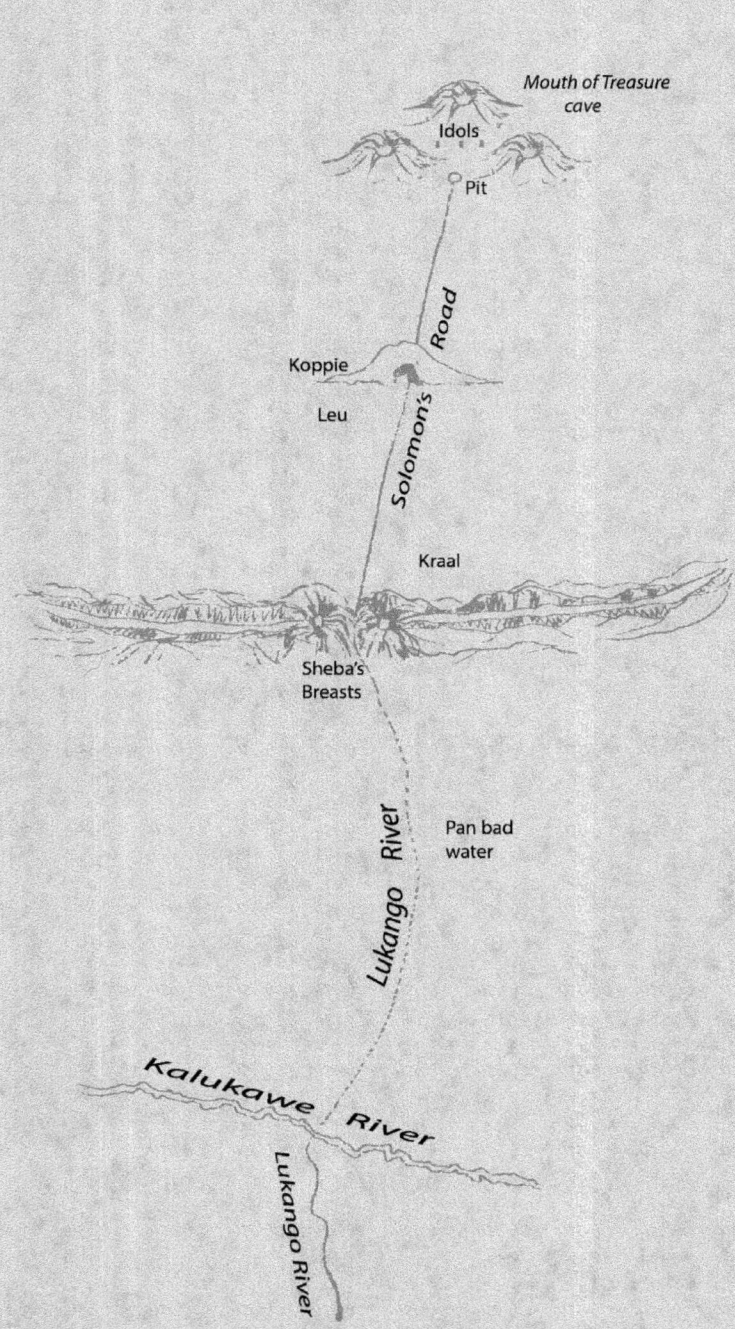

I don't know,' I said, 'I know where they are said to be. Once I saw the peaks of the mountains that border them, but there were a hundred and thirty miles of desert between me and them, and I am not aware that any white man ever got across it except one.'

I agreed to lead this expedition through a mysterious map, something I would have never done just to share a part of a treasure, but such reasons were a rare privilege in our profession. The least I would expect of not returning alive was that my son would be taken care of with a handsome stipend.

We were also joined by Umbopa who seemed to be more distinguished than the other porters of his class.

We lost one of our servants during an elephant hunt. Our journey continued through a desert. Craving for water to quench our thirst we reached a mountain range called Suliman Berg, across Sheba's Breasts. There, in a cave, we found the frozen corpse of a sixteenth-century Portuguese explorer, José Silvestre, who had drawn the map with his own blood. That night we lost another servant, Hottentot Ventvögel, and Sir Henry decided to bury him near Silvestra's body.

'Let us go,' said Sir Henry in a low voice, 'stay, we will give him a companion,' and lifting up the dead body of Hottentot Ventvögel, he placed it near the old Dom. Then he stooped, and with a jerk broke the rotten string of the crucifix, which hung round da Silvestra's neck, for his fingers were too cold to attempt to unfasten it.

Then leaving these two, the proud white man of a past age, and the poor Hottentot, we crept out of the cave into the welcome sunshine and resumed our path.

We then reached a lush, green plateau called, Kukuanaland, the capital of which was Loo. The people there spoke an ancient language known as Zulu. When Captain Good played around with his set of false teeth the Kukuanas retaliated in fear. We came across their warriors who almost killed us, if we did not portray ourselves as 'white men from the stars' and time and again continued to prove our divinity.

Kukuana was ruled by a violent and unchallenged king, Twala. He was known to have

murdered
his brother and
of mercilessly leaving
his brother's wife and son,
Ignosi, in the desert to die.
Gagool, his chief adviser, was known for witch hunting and murdering alleged traitors without an opportunity for justification.

A rebellion in which we participated broke out when it was revealed that Umbopa was in fact, Ignosi. more so as the true ruler of Kukuanaland. The arrangements for attack thus briefly indicated were set in motion with a rapidity that spoke well for the perfection of the Kukuana military system. Within little more than an hour rations had been served out, the divisions were formed and the scheme of onslaught was explained to the leaders. The whole force, numbering about 18,000 men, was ready to move, with the exception of a guard left in charge of the wounded.

Good came up to Sir Henry and myself.

'Goodbye, you fellows,' he said, 'I am off with the right wing according to orders; and so I have come to shake hands, in case we should not meet again, you know,' he added significantly.

We shook hands in silence.

'It is business,' said Sir Henry, his deep voice shaking a little, 'and I confess I never expect to see tomorrow's sun. So far as I can make out, the Greys, with whom I am to go, are to fight until they are wiped out in order to outflank Twala. Well, so be it; at any rate, it will be a man's death. Goodbye, old fellow. God bless you! I hope you will pull through and live to collar the diamonds; but if you do, take my advice and don't have anything more to do with Pretenders!'

Infadoos, who was a wary old general, and knew the absolute importance of keeping up the spirits of his men on the eve of such a desperate encounter, addressed his own regiment, the Greys, in a poetical language. He explained to them the honour that they were receiving in being put thus in the forefront of the battle. He promised large rewards of cattle and promotion to all who survived in the event of Ignosi's arms being successful.

Never before had I seen such an absolute devotion to the idea of duty, and such a complete indifference to its bitter fruits.

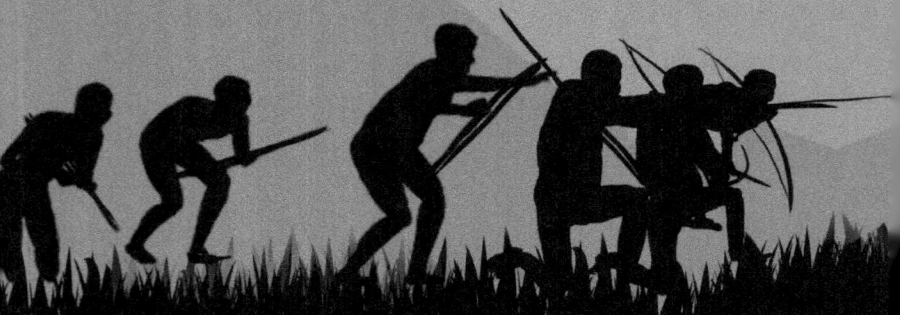

During the battle, Sir Henry found themselves facing each other. They engaged in a brutal and vicious attack. Sir Henry gashed Twala in his shoulder. There was a shriek of excitement from a thousand throats, and, behold! Twala's head seemed to spring from his shoulders: then it fell and came rolling and bounding along the ground towards Ignosi, stopping just at his feet. For a second the corpse stood upright; then with a dull crash it came to the earth, and the gold torque from its neck rolled away across the pavement. As it did so, Sir Henry, overpowered by faintness and loss of blood, fell heavily across the body of the dead king.

In a second, he was lifted up, and eager hands were pouring water on his face. Another minute, and the grey eyes opened wide.

He was not dead.

Then I, just as the sun sank, stepping to where Twala's head lay in the dust, unloosed the diamond from the dead brows, and handed it to Ignosi.

'Take it,' I said, 'lawful king of the Kukuanas—king by birth and victory.'

'Now,' he began, 'now our rebellion is swallowed up in victory, and our evil-doing is justified by strength.

'In the morning the oppressors arose and stretched themselves; they bound on their harness and made them ready to war.

'They rose up and tossed their spears: the soldiers called to the captains, "Come, lead us"—and the captains cried to the king, "You direct the battle."

'They laughed in their pride, twenty thousand men, and yet a twenty thousand.

'Their plumes covered the valleys as the plumes of a bird cover her nest; they shook their shields and shouted, yeah, they shook their shields in the sunlight; they lusted for battle and were glad.

'They came up against me; their strong ones ran swiftly to slay me; they cried, "Ha! ha! he is as one already dead."

'My lightning pierced them; I licked up their strength with the lightning of my spears; I shook them to the ground with the thunder of my shouting.

'They broke—they scattered—they were gone as the mists of the morning.

'They are food for the kites and the foxes, and the place of battle is fat with their blood.

'Where are the mighty ones who rose up in the morning?

'Where are the proud ones who tossed their spears and cried, 'He is as a man already dead'?

'They bow their heads, but not in sleep; they are stretched out, but not in sleep.

'They are forgotten; they have gone into the blackness; they dwell in the dead moons; others shall lead away their wives, and their children shall remember them no more.

'And I—! the king—like an eagle I have found my eyrie.

'Behold! Far have I flown in the night season, yet have I returned to my young at the daybreak.

'Shelter ye under the shadow of my wings, O people, and I will comfort you, and ye shall not be dismayed.

'Now is the good time, the time of spoil.

'The winter is overpast with storms, the summer is come with flowers.

'Now Evil shall cover up her face, now Mercy and Gladness shall dwell in the land.

'Rejoice, rejoice, my people!

'Let all the stars rejoice in that this tyranny is trodden down, in that I am the king.'

Ignosi stopped his song, and out of the gathering gloom came back the deep reply—

'You are the king!'

After the fight was ended, Sir Henry and Good were carried into Twala's hut, where I joined them. They were both utterly exhausted by exertion and loss of blood, and, indeed, my own condition was little better. I could stand more fatigue than most men, probably on account of my light weight and long training; but that night I was quite done up. Also my head was aching violently from a blow I had received in the morning.

With the help of Foulata, who worked for us as a handmaiden, and especially Good, we managed to get off the chain shirts, which had certainly saved the lives of two of us that day. As I expected, we found that the flesh underneath was terribly torn, for though the steel links had kept the weapons from entering, they had not prevented them from bruising. As a remedy Foulata brought us some pounded green leaves, with an aromatic odour, which, when applied as a plaster, gave us considerable relief.

A few days later, we set off to King Solomon's Mines, with an old lady named Gagool who was ordered to lead us there. Our party consisted of our three selves and Foulata, who waited on us—especially on Good—Infadoos, Gagool, and a party of guards and attendants. Our excitement was so intense, as we saw the way to Solomon's treasure chamber thrown open at last, that I for one began to tremble and shake.

A few yards down the passage, in the narrow way through the rock, Gagool had paused, and was waiting for us.

Here Foulata said that she felt faint and could go no farther, but would wait there. Accordingly, we set her down on the unfinished wall, placing the basket of provisions by her side, and left her to recover.

Following the passage for about fifteen paces farther, we came suddenly to an elaborately painted wooden door. It was standing wide open. Whoever was last there had either not found the time to shut it, or had forgotten to do so.

'Hee! Hee! white men,' sniggered Gagool, as the light from the lamp fell upon it. 'What did I tell you, that the white man who came here fled in haste, and dropped the woman's bag—behold it! Look within also and you will find a water-gourd amongst the stones.'

Good stooped down and lifted it. It was heavy and jingled.

'By Jove! I believe it's full of diamonds,' he said, in an awed whisper; and, indeed, the idea of a small goatskin full of diamonds is enough to awe anybody.

'Go on,' said Sir Henry impatiently. 'Here, old lady, give me the lamp,' and taking it from Gagool's hand, he stepped through the doorway and held it high above his head.

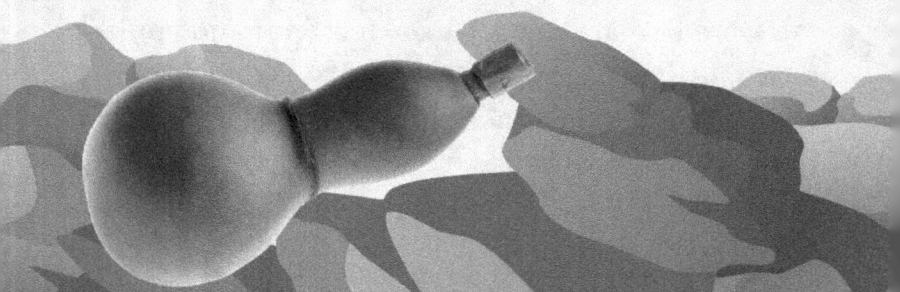

We pressed in after him, forgetful for the moment of the bag of diamonds, and found ourselves in King Solomon's treasure chamber.

'There are the diamonds,' I cried.

'Open the other chests, white men,' said Gagool, 'there are surely more therein. Take your fill, white lords! Ha! Ha! Take your fill.'

Thus requested, we set to work to pull up the stone lids on the other two, first—not without a feeling of sacrilege—breaking the seals that fastened them. Hoorah! They were full too, full to the brim.

What we did not see, however, was the unfaithful look old Gagool favoured us with as she crept, crept like a snake, out of the treasure chamber and down the passage towards the door of solid rock.

Hark! Cry upon cry came ringing up the vaulted path. It was Foulata's voice!

'Oh, Bougwan! Help! Help! The stone falls!'

'Leave go, girl! Then—'

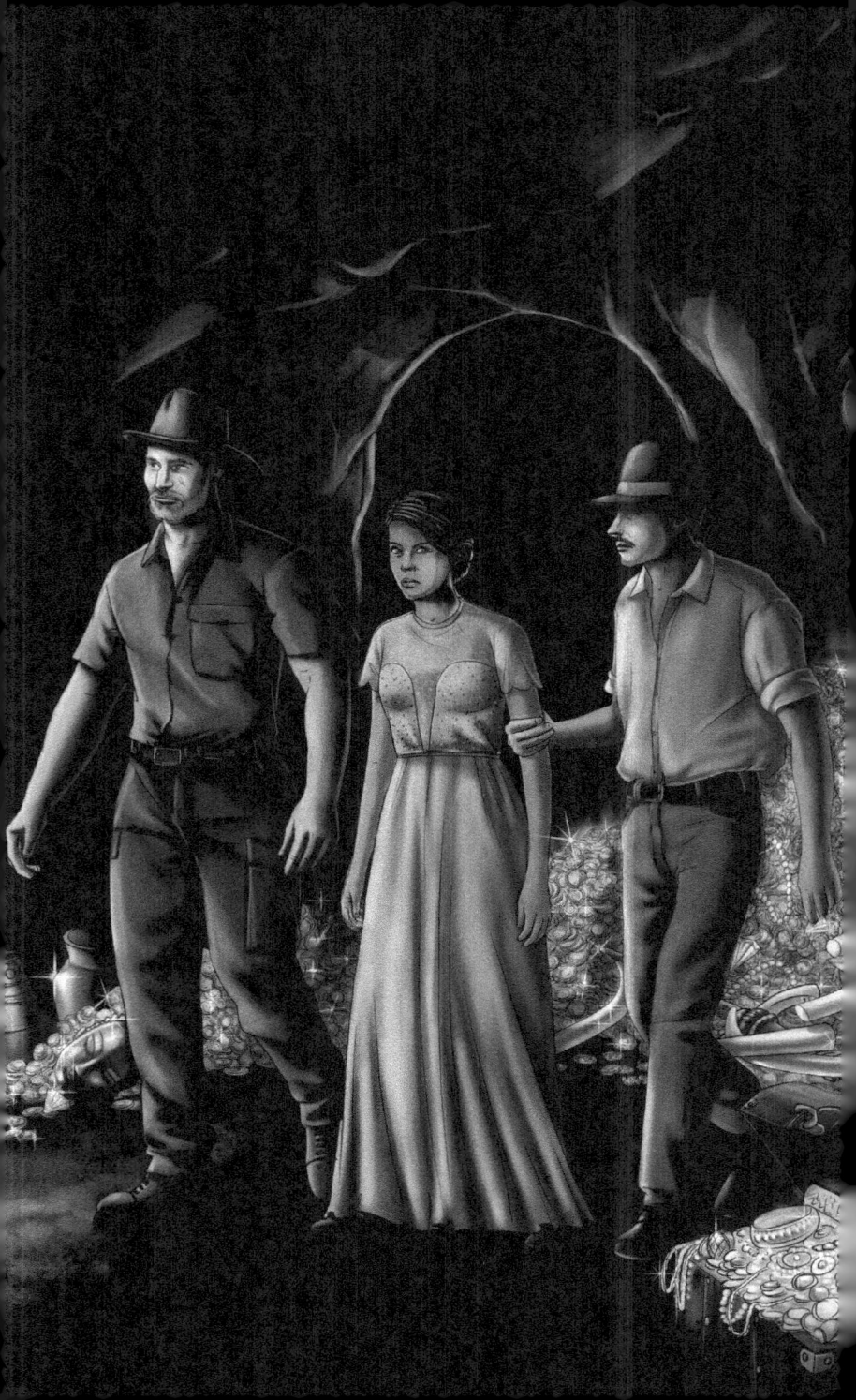

'Help! Help! She has stabbed me!'

The poor girl was stabbed in the body, and I saw that she could not live long.

Later Gagool got crushed under the stone door of the mine. We were now in a dark chamber with dwindling food and water supplies. Our survival was at risk until we found an escape route after many attempts. We carried sufficient amount of diamonds on our return that would lead us well for life. We bade farewell and took a different route back.

And now I come to perhaps the strangest adventure that happened to us in all this strange business, and one which showed how wonderfully things were brought about.

I was walking along quietly, some way in front of the other two, down the banks of the stream, which ran from the oasis until it was swallowed up in the hungry desert sands, when suddenly I stopped and rubbed my eyes, as well I might. There, not twenty yards in front of me, placed in a charming situation, under the shade of a species of fig tree, and facing to the stream, was a cosy hut, with grass and withes, but having a full-length door instead of a bee-hole.

'What the dickens,' said I to myself, 'can a hut be doing here?' Even as I said it the door of the hut opened, and there limped out of it a white man clothed in skins, and with an enormous black beard. I thought that I must have got a touch of the sun. It was impossible. No hunter ever came to such a place as this. Certainly no hunter would ever settle in it. I stared and stared, and so did the other man, and just at that juncture Sir Henry and Good walked up.

'Look here, you fellows,' I said, 'is that a white man, or am I mad?'

Sir Henry looked, and Good looked, and then all of a sudden the lame white man with a black beard uttered a great cry, and began hobbling towards us. When he was close he fell down in a sort of faint.

With a spring Sir Henry was by his side.

'Great Powers!' he cried, 'it is my brother George!'

'My dear old fellow,' burst out Sir Henry at last, 'I thought you were dead. I have been over Solomon's Mountains to find you. I had given up all hope of ever seeing you again, and now I come across you perched in the desert.'

'I tried to cross Solomon's Mountains nearly two years ago, but when I reached here a boulder fell on my leg and crushed it, and I have been able to go neither forward nor back.'

Then I came up.

'How do you do, Mr Neville?' I said, 'do you remember me?'

'Why,' he said, 'isn't it Hunter Quatermain, and Good too? Hold on a minute, you fellows, I am getting dizzy again. It is all so very strange, and, when a man has ceased to hope, so very happy!'

That evening, over the campfire, George Curtis told us his story, which, in its way, was almost as eventful as our own, and, put shortly, amounted to this. A little less than two years before, he had started from Sitanda's Kraal, to try to reach Suliman's Berg. As for the note I had sent him by Jim, and he had never heard of it till today. But, acting upon information he had received from the natives, he headed not for Sheba's Breasts, but for the ladder-like descent of the mountains down which we had just come, which was clearly a better route than that marked out in old Dom Silvestra's plan. In the desert, he and Jim had suffered great hardships, but finally they reached this oasis, where a terrible accident befell George Curtis. On the day of their arrival he was sitting by the stream, and Jim was extracting the honey from the nest of a stingless bee which is to be found in the desert, on the top of a bank immediately above him. In so doing he loosened a great boulder of rock, which fell upon George Curtis right leg, crushing it frightfully. From that day he had been so lame that he found it impossible to go either forward or back, and had preferred to take the chances of dying in the oasis to the certainty of perishing in the desert.

As for food, however, they got on pretty well, for they had a good supply of ammunition, and the oasis was frequented, especially at night, by large quantities of game, which came thither for water. These they shot, or trapped in pitfalls, using the flesh for food, and, after their clothes wore out, the hides for clothing.

'And so,' George Curtis said, 'we have lived for nearly two years, like a second Robinson Crusoe and his man Friday, hoping against hope that some natives might come here to help us away, but none have come. Only last night we settled that Jim should leave me, and try to reach Sitanda's Kraal to get assistance. He was to go tomorrow, but I had little hope of ever seeing him back again. And now you, of all people in the world, you, who, as I fancied, had long ago forgotten all about me, and were living comfortably in old England, turn up in a promiscuous way and find me where you least expected. It is the most wonderful thing that I have ever heard of, and the most merciful too.'

Here, at this point, I think that I shall end my history. Our journey across the desert back to Sitanda's Kraal was most strenuous, especially as we had to support George Curtis. His right leg was very weak indeed, and continually threw out splinters of bone. But we did accomplish it somehow, and to give its details would only be to reproduce much of what happened to us on the former occasion.

Six months from the date of our arrival at Sitanda's, we found our guns and other goods quite safe. Then I bid farewell to all who have accompanied me through the strangest trip I ever made in the course of a long and varied experience.

PS—Just as I had written the last word, a Kafir came up my avenue of orange trees, carrying a letter in a cleft stick, which he had brought from the post. It turned out to be from Sir Henry, and as it speaks for itself I give it in full.

October 1, 1884.

Brayley Hall, Yorkshire.

My Dear Quatermain,

I send you a line a few mails back to say that the three of us, George, Good, and myself, fetched up all right in England. We got off the boat at Southampton, and went up to town. You should have seen what a swell Good turned out the very next day, beautifully shaved, frock coat fitting like a glove, brand new eye-glass, etc, etc. I went and walked in the park with him, where I met some people I know, and at once told them the story of his 'beautiful white legs.'

He is furious, especially as some ill-natured person has printed it in a Society paper.

To come to business, Good and I took the diamonds to Streeter's to be valued, as we arranged, and really I am afraid to tell you what they put them at, it seems so enormous. They say that of course, it is more or less guess-work, as such stones have never to their knowledge been put on the market in anything like such quantities. It appears that (with the exception of one or two of the largest) they are of the finest water, and equal in every way to the best Brazilian stones. I asked them if they would buy them, but they said that it was beyond their power to do so, and recommended us to sell by degrees, over a period of years indeed, for fear lest we should flood the market. They offer, however, a hundred and eighty thousand for a very small portion of them.

You must come home, Quatermain, and see about these things, especially if you insist upon making the magnificent present of the third share, which does not belong to me, to my brother George. As for Good, he is no good. His time is too much occupied in shaving, and other matters connected with the vain adorning of the body. But I think he is still down on his luck about Foulata. He told me that since he had been home he hadn't seen a woman to touch her, either as regards her figure or the sweetness of her expression.

I want you to come home, my dear old comrade, and to buy a house near here. You have done your day's work, and have lots of money now, and there is a place for sale quite close which would suit you admirably. Do come; the sooner the better; you can finish writing the story of our adventures on board ship. We have refused to tell the tale till it is written by you, for fear lest we shall not be believed. If you start on receipt of this you will reach here by Christmas, and I book you to stay with me for that. Good is coming, and George; and so, by the way, is your boy Harry (there's a bribe for you). I have had him down for a week's shooting, and like him. He is a cool young hand; he shot me in the leg, cut out the pellets, and then remarked upon the advantages of having a medical student with every shooting party!

Goodbye, old boy; I can't say any more, but I know that you will come, if it is only to oblige.

Your sincere friend,

Henry Curtis.

PS—The axe with which I chopped off Twala's head is fixed above my writing-table. I wish that we could have managed to bring away the coats of chain armour. Don't lose poor Foulata's basket in which you brought away the diamonds.

HC

Today is Tuesday. There is a steamer going on

Friday. I really think that I must take Curtis at his word, and sail by her for England, if it is only to see you, Harry, my boy, and to look after the printing of this history, which is a task that I do not like to trust to anybody else.

ALLAN QUATERMAIN.

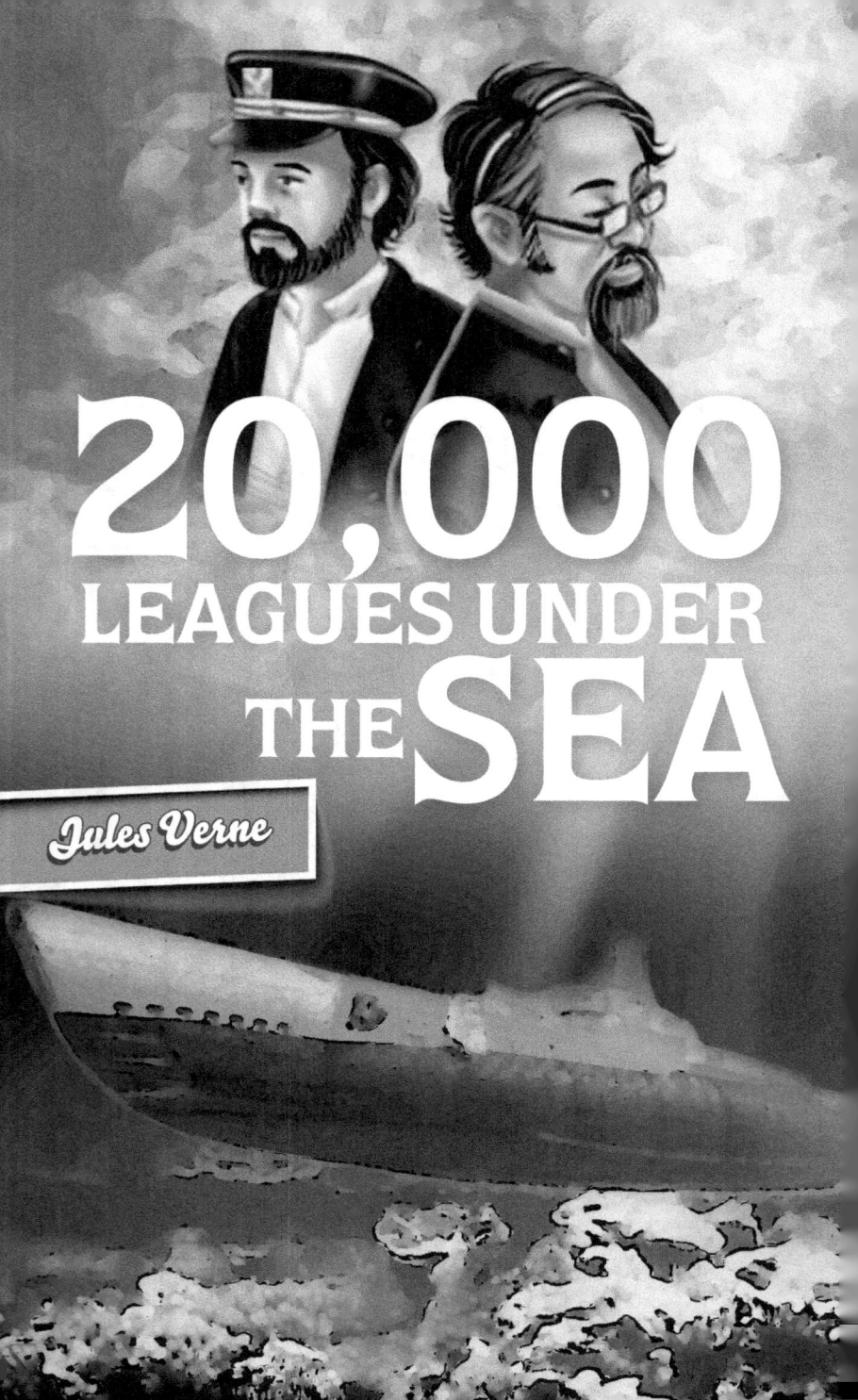

The year 1866 was signalized by a remarkable incident, a mysterious and puzzling phenomenon, which no one has yet forgotten. Traders, sailors, crew members and sea captains, from Europe and North America, as well as naval officers and government officials of several countries from the two continents, were deeply interested in the matter.

For some time past vessels had been met by 'an enormous thing,' a long object, spindle-shaped, occasionally phosphorescent, and infinitely larger and more rapid in its movements than a whale. It was a mysterious sea monster that some people called it a Narwhal.

On 20 July 1866, the steamer *Governor Higginson,* of the Calcutta and Burnach Steam Navigation Company, had met this moving mass five miles off the east coast of Australia.

Similar facts were observed on 23 July in the same year—in the Pacific Ocean, by the *Columbus,* of the West India and Pacific Steam Navigation Company.

Fifteen days later, two thousand miles farther off, the *Helvetia,* of the Compagnie-Nationale, and the *Shannon*, of the Royal Mail Steamship Company, sailing to windward in that portion of the Atlantic lying between the United States and

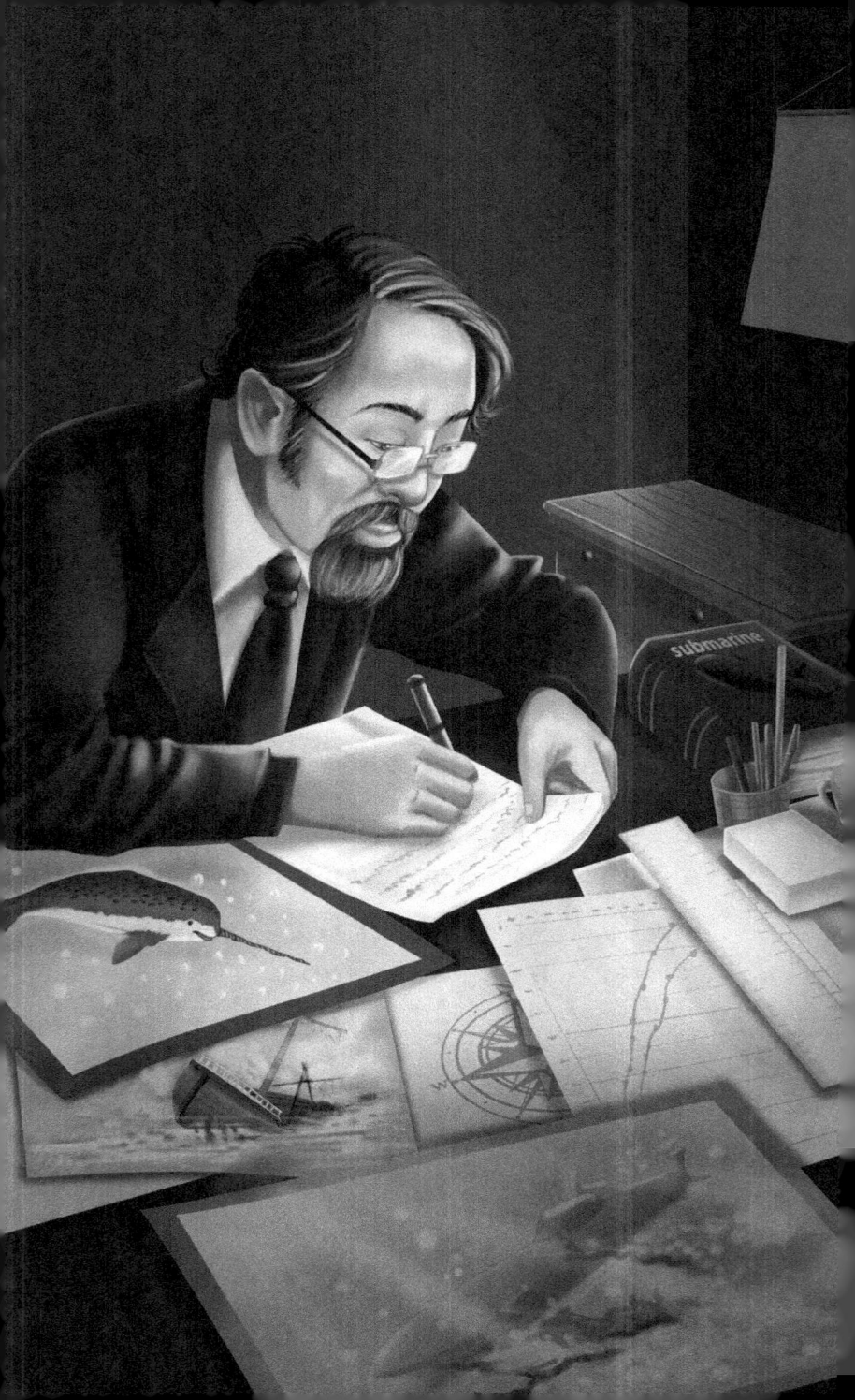

Europe, respectively, signalled the monster to each other in 42° 15' N. lat. and 60° 35' W. long. In these simultaneous observations, they justified in estimating the minimum length of the mammal at more than 350, as the *Shannon* and *Helvetia* were of smaller dimensions than it was, though they measured three hundred feet over all.

At the period when these events took place, I had just returned from a scientific research in Nebraska, in the United States.

Upon my arrival in New York, several persons did me the honour of consulting me on the phenomenon in question. I was obliged to explain myself point by point. I discussed the question in all its forms, politically and scientifically; and I give here an extract from a carefully studied article, which I published on 30 April. It ran as follows:

'After examining one by one the different theories, rejecting all other suggestions, it becomes necessary to admit the existence of a marine animal of enormous power.

'We do know all living kinds, we must necessarily seek for the animal in question amongst those marine beings already classed; and, in that case, I should be disposed to admit the existence of a gigantic Narwhal.'

My article was warmly discussed, which procured it a high reputation.

The industrial and commercial papers treated the question chiefly from this point of view. Public opinion had been pronounced. The United States were the first in the field; and in New York, they prepared for an expedition destined to pursue this Narwhal. A frigate of great speed, the *Abraham Lincoln*, was put in commission as soon as possible. The arsenals were opened to Commander Farragut, who hastened the arming of his frigate; but, as it always happens, the moment it was decided to pursue the monster, it did not ever appear. For two months, no one heard it spoken of. No ship met the Narwhal. It seemed as if this unicorn knew of the plots weaving around it.

So, when the frigate had been armed for a long campaign, and provided with formidable fishing apparatus, no one could tell what course to pursue. Impatience grew apace, when, on 2 July, they learned that a steamer of the line of San Francisco, from California to Shanghai, had seen the animal three weeks before in the North Pacific Ocean. The excitement caused by this news was extreme. The ship was well stocked with coal.

Three hours before the *Abraham Lincoln* left Brooklyn pier, I received a letter worded as follows:

To
M ARONNAX,
Professor in the Museum of Paris,
Fifth Avenue Hotel,
New York.

Sir,
If you will consent to join the Abraham Lincoln in this expedition, the Government of the United States will with pleasure see France represented in the enterprise.

Commander Farragut has a cabin at your disposal.

Very cordially yours,
JB HOBSON,
Secretary of Marine.

Three seconds before the arrival of JB Hobson's letter, I no more thought of pursuing the unicorn than of attempting the passage of the North Sea. Three seconds after reading the letter of the honourable Secretary of Marine, I felt that my true vocation, the sole end of my life, was to chase this disturbing monster and get rid of it from the world. Conseil, my servant who always travelled with me, accompanied us.

The *Abraham Lincoln* wanted for no means of destruction; and, what was better still she had on board Ned Land, the prince of harpooners. Ned Land was a Canadian, with an uncommon quickness of hand, and who knew no equal in his dangerous occupation. Skill, coolness, audacity, and cunning he possessed in a superior degree, and it must be a cunning whale to escape the stroke of his harpoon.

We set off into the Pacific Ocean and soon enough discovered the monster. Initially some of us mistook it for a mass of phosphoric particles, but it was clearly not. All of us aboard the ship had gathered when the monster started trying to sheer off and the animal was approaching with a velocity double her own. A direct collision could have been a disaster.

During the frenzied attack, Ned, Conseil and I found ourselves thrown into the ocean without our ship. We almost gave ourselves up to be dead, when we realized we had floated on top of the monster — whose skin was in fact steel! A few hours later, eight men opened a hatch and dragged us into the submarine which we found was named the *Nautilus*. Its captain, Captain Nemo, had his own terms and conditions for the prisoners.

'I have hesitated,' said he, 'but I have thought that my interest might be reconciled with that pity to which every human being has a right. You will remain on board my vessel, since fate has cast you there. You will be free; and, in exchange for this liberty, I shall only impose one single condition. Your word of honour to submit to it will suffice.'

'Speak, sir,' I answered. 'I suppose this condition is one which a man of honour may accept?'

'Yes, sir; it is this: it is possible that certain events, unforeseen, may oblige me to consign you to your cabins for some hours or some days, as

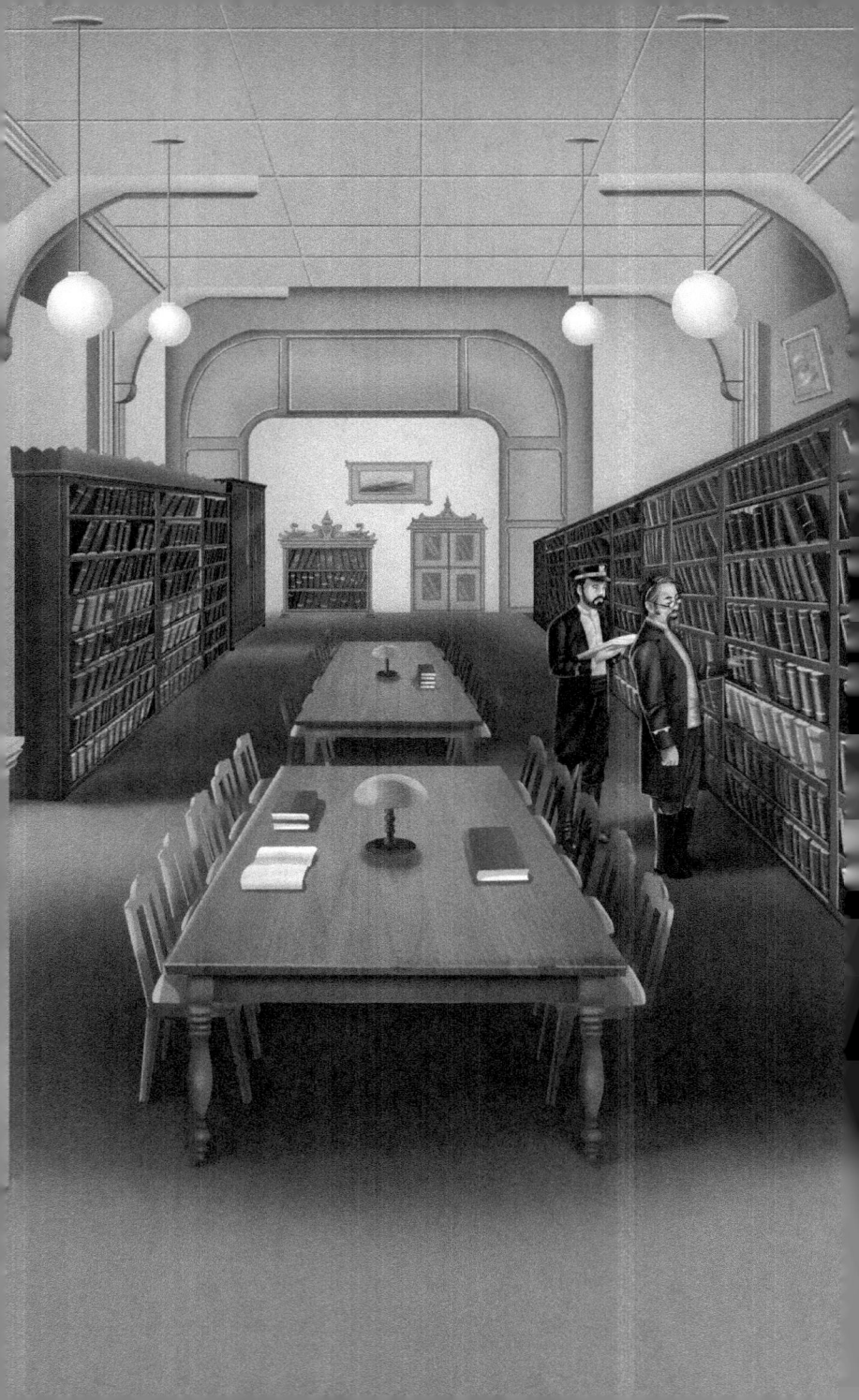

the case may be. As I desire never to use violence, I expect from you, more than all the others, a passive obedience. In thus acting, I take all the responsibility: I acquit you entirely, for I make it an impossibility for you to see what ought not to be seen. Do you accept this condition?'

Then things took place on board which, to say the least, were singular, and which ought not to be seen by people who were not placed beyond the pale of social laws. Amongst the surprises, which the future was preparing for me, this might not be the least.

'We accept,' I said, 'only I will ask your permission, sir, to address one question to you—one only.'

'Speak, sir.'

'You said that we should be free on board.'

'Entirely.'

'I ask you, then, what do you mean by this liberty?'

'Just the liberty to go, to come, to see, to observe even all that passes here save under rare circumstances—the liberty, in short, which we enjoy ourselves, my companions and I.'

It was evident that we did not understand one another.

'Pardon me, sir,' I resumed, 'but this liberty is only what every prisoner has of pacing his prison. It cannot suffice us.'

'It must suffice you, however.'

'What! We must renounce forever seeing our country, our friends and our relations again?'

'Yes, sir. But to renounce that unendurable worldly yoke which men believe to be liberty is not perhaps as painful as you think.'

'Well,' said Ned Land, 'never will I give my word of honour not to try to escape.'

'I did not ask you for your word of honour, Master Land,' answered the commander, coldly.

'Sir,' I replied, beginning to get angry in spite of myself, 'you abuse your situation towards us; it is cruelty.'

'No, sir, it is mercy. You are my prisoners of war. I keep you, when I could, by a word, plunge you into the depths of the ocean. You attacked me. You came to surprise a secret which no man in the world must penetrate—the secret of my whole existence. And you think that I am going to send you back to that world which must know me no more? Never! In retaining you, it is not you whom I guard—it is myself.'

These words indicated a resolution taken on the part of the commander, against which no arguments would prevail.

'So, sir,' I rejoined, 'you give us simply the choice between life and death?'

'Simply.'

'My friends,' said I, 'to a question thus put, there is nothing to answer. But no word of honour binds us to the master of this vessel.'

'None, sir,' answered the unknown.

Then, in a gentler tone, he continued,

'Now, permit me to finish what I have to say to you. I know you, M Aronnax. You and your companions will not, perhaps, have so much to complain of in the chance, which has bound you to my fate. You will find amongst the books, which are my favourite study the work which you have published on the great depths of the sea. I have often read it. You have carried out your work as far as terrestrial science permits you. But you do not know all—you have not seen all. Let me tell you then, professor, that you will not regret the time passed on board my vessel. You are going to visit the land of marvels.'

Captain Nemo had exiled himself from the remainder of the world, since his family was affected in an encounter with the enemy forces that had taken over his country. He had a life of his own in the submarine and wouldn't ever allow that to be disturbed or exposed.

Amongst the many adventures, Captain Nemo sent an invitation for a hunt to the Island of Crespo, a submarine forest, which was through a walk through the waters.

How can I retrace the impression left upon me by that walk under the waters? Words are impotent to relate such wonders! Captain Nemo walked in front and his companion followed some steps behind. Conseil and I remained near each other, as if an exchange of words had been possible through our metallic cases. I no longer felt the weight of my clothing, or of my shoes, of my reservoir of air, or

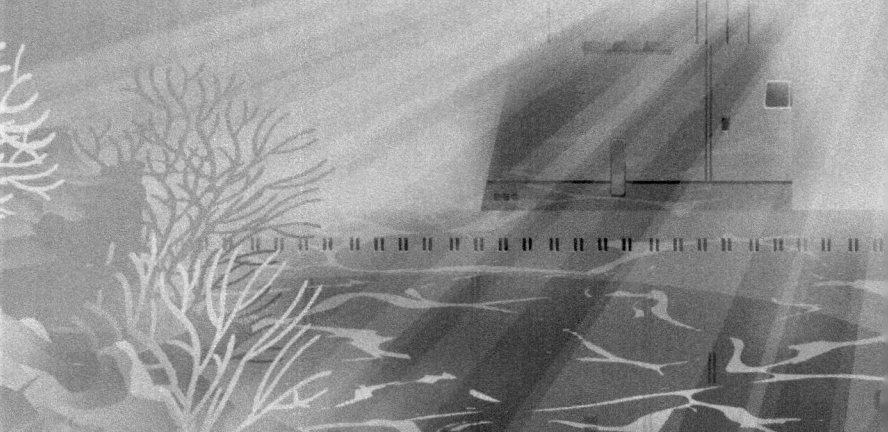

my thick helmet, in the midst of which my head rattled like an almond in its shell.

The light, which lit the soil thirty feet below the surface of the ocean, astonished me by its power. The solar rays shone through the watery mass easily, and dissipated all colour, and I clearly distinguished objects at a distance of a 150 yards. Beyond that the tints darkened into fine gradations of ultramarine, and faded into vague obscurity. Truly this water which surrounded me was but another air denser than the terrestrial atmosphere, but almost as transparent. Above me was the calm surface of the sea. We were walking on fine, even sand, not wrinkled, as on a flat shore, which retained the impression of the billows. This dazzling carpet, really a reflector, repelled the rays of the sun with wonderful intensity, which accounted for the vibration, which penetrated every atom of liquid. Shall I be believed when I say that, at the depth of thirty feet, I could see as if I was in broad daylight?

For a quarter of an hour I trod on this sand, sown with the impalpable dust of shells. The hull of the *Nautilus*, resembling a long shoal, disappeared by degrees; but its lantern, when darkness should overtake us in the waters, would help to guide us on board by its distinct rays.

Soon forms of objects outlined in the distance were discernible. I recognized magnificent rocks, hung with a tapestry of zoophytes of the most beautiful kind, and I was at first struck by the peculiar effect of this medium.

It was then ten in the morning; the rays of the sun struck the surface of the waves at rather an oblique angle, and at the touch of their light, decomposed by refraction as through a prism, flowers, rocks, plants, shells and polypi were shaded at the edges by the seven solar colours. It was marvellous, a feast for the eyes, this complication of coloured tints, a perfect kaleidoscope of green, yellow, orange, violet, indigo and blue; in one word, the whole palette of an enthusiastic colourist! Why could I not communicate to Conseil the lively sensations, which were mounting to my brain, and rival him in expressions of admiration? For nothing I knew, Captain Nemo and his companion might be able to exchange thoughts by means of signs previously agreed upon. So, for want of better, I talked to myself; I declaimed in the copper box which covered my head, thereby expending more air in vain words than was perhaps wise.

Various kinds of isis, clusters of pure tuft-coral, prickly fungi, and anemones formed a brilliant garden of flowers, decked with their collarettes of blue tentacles, sea-stars studding the sandy bottom. It was a real grief to me to crush under my feet the brilliant specimens of molluscs, which strewed the ground by thousands, of hammerheads, donaciae (veritable bounding shells), of staircases, and red helmet-shells, angel-wings, and many others produced by this inexhaustible ocean. But we were bound to walk, so we went on, whilst above our heads waved medusae whose umbrellas of opal or rose-pink, escalloped with a band of blue, sheltered us from the rays of the sun and fiery pelagiae, which, in the darkness, would have strewn our path with phosphorescent light.

All these wonders I saw in the space of a quarter of a mile, scarcely stopping, and following Captain Nemo, who beckoned me on by signs. Soon the nature of the soil changed; to the sandy plain succeeded an extent of slimy mud which the Americans call 'ooze,' composed of equal parts of silicious and calcareous shells. We then travelled over a plain of seaweed of wild and luxuriant vegetation. This sward was of close texture, and soft to the feet, and rivalled the softest carpet woven by the hand of man. But whilst verdure was spread at our feet, it did not abandon our heads. A light network of marine plants, of that inexhaustible family of seaweeds of which more than two thousand kinds are known, grew on the surface of the water.

While we were on the *Nautilus,* we hunted and visited Atlantis, the ancient land of Meropis mentioned by the historian Theopompus, and whose very existence was denied by many philosophers. However, it was an island of angry natives, who fished for giant pearls. While we were there, men were asked to return to the cells and were given sleeping pills. Later I was asked to nurse a man who was injured and then died, later he was buried where many other were laid.

Soon we took off for a place that only Captain Nemo seemed to know the purpose of. Upon reaching the spot, the Captain merely said, 'It is here'. I looked out of my submarine to see the wreck of an ancient ship. It certainly belonged to past times. The Captain revealed that the name of this vessel was the *Avenger*. The way of describing this unlooked-for scene, the history of the patriot ship, told at first so coldly, and the emotion with which this Captain Nemo pronounced the name of the *Avenger*, the significance of which could not escape me, all impressed itself deeply on my mind. The future would soon teach me that. But the *Nautilus* was rising slowly to the surface of the sea, and the form of the *Avenger* disappeared by degrees from my sight. Soon a slight rolling told me that we were in the open air. At that moment, a dull boom was heard. I looked at the captain. He did not move.

'What is that ship, Ned?'

'By its rigging and the height of its lower masts,' said the Canadian, 'I bet she is a ship-of-war. May it reach us; and, if necessary, sink this cursed *Nautilus*.'

'Friend Ned,' replied Conseil, 'what harm can it do to the *Nautilus*? Can it attack beneath the waves? Can its cannonade attack us at the bottom of the sea?'

'Tell me, Ned,' I said, 'can you recognize what country she belongs to?'

The Canadian knitted his eyebrows, dropped his eyelids and screwed up the corners of his eyes, and for a few moments fixed a piercing look upon the vessel.

'No, sir,' he replied, 'I cannot tell what nation she belongs to, for she shows no colours. But I can declare she is a man-of-war, for a long flag flutters from her main mast.'

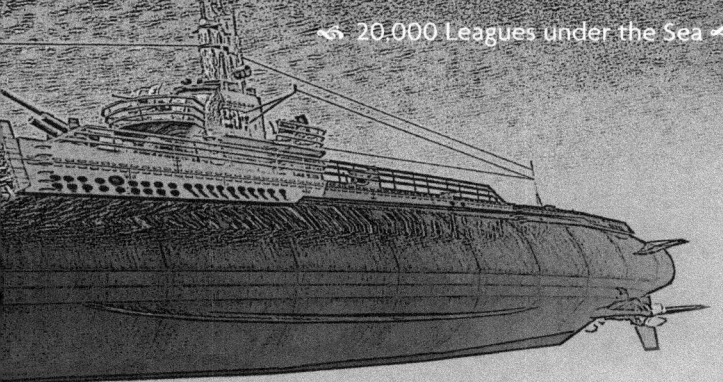

'Sir,' said Ned Land, 'if that vessel passes within a mile of us I shall throw myself into the sea, and I should advise you to do the same.'

I did not reply to the Canadian's suggestion, but continued watching the ship. Whether English, French, American or Russian, she would be sure to take us in if we could only reach her. Presently a white smoke burst from the fore part of the vessel; some seconds after, the water, agitated by the fall of a heavy body, splashed the stern of the *Nautilus,* and shortly afterwards a loud explosion struck my ear.

'What! they are firing at us!' I exclaimed.

'So please you, sir,' said Ned, 'they have recognized the unicorn, and they are firing at us.'

'But,' I said, 'surely they can see that there are men in the case?'

'It is, perhaps, because of that,' replied Ned Land, looking at me.

On the fore part of the platform, Captain Nemo unfurled a black flag, similar to the one he had placed at the South Pole. In that moment a shot struck the shell of the *Nautilus* obliquely, without piercing it; and, rebounding near the captain, it disappeared into the sea. He shrugged his shoulders; and, addressing me, said shortly, 'Go down, you and your companions, go down!'

'Sir,' I cried, 'are you going to attack this vessel?'

'Sir, I am going to sink it.'

'You will not do that?'

'I shall do it,' he replied coldly. 'And I advise you not to judge me, Sir. Fate has shown you what you ought not to have seen. The attack has begun; go down.'

'What is this vessel?'

'You do not know? Very well! So much the better! Its nationality to you, at least, will be a secret. Go down!'

We could but obey. About fifteen of the sailors surrounded the captain, looking with unforgiving hatred at the vessel nearing them. One could feel that the same desire of vengeance animated every soul. When I went down in the moment, another projectile struck the *Nautilus,* and I heard the captain exclaimed, 'Strike, mad vessel! Shower your useless shot! And then, you will not escape the spur of the *Nautilus*. But it is not here that you shall perish! I would not have your ruins mingle with those of the *Avenger*!'

I cast a last look at the man-of-war, which was putting on steam, and rejoined Ned and Conseil.

'We will fly!' I said.

'Good!' said Ned. 'What is this vessel?'

'I do not know; but, whatever it is, it will be sunk before night. In any case, it is better to perish with it, than be made accomplices in a retaliation the justice of which we cannot judge.'

'That is my opinion too,' said Ned Land, coolly. 'Let us wait for night.'

At three in the morning, with full of uneasiness, I mounted the platform. Captain Nemo was standing at the fore part near his flag, which a slight breeze displayed above his head. He did not take his eyes from the vessel. The intensity of his look seemed to attract, and fascinate, and draw it onward more surely than if he had been towing it. The moon was then passing the meridian. Jupiter was rising in the east. Amid this peaceful scene of nature, sky and ocean rivalled each other in tranquillity, the sea offering to the orbs of night the finest mirror they could ever have in which to reflect their image. As I thought of the deep calm of these elements, compared with all those passions brooding imperceptibly within the *Nautilus,* I shuddered.

The vessel was within two miles of us. It was ever nearing that phosphorescent light which showed the presence of the *Nautilus*. I could see its green and red lights, and its white lantern hanging from the large foremast. An indistinct vibration quivered through its rigging, showing that the furnaces were heated to the uttermost. Sheaves of sparks and red ashes flew from the funnels, shining in the atmosphere like stars.

I remained thus until six in the morning, without Captain Nemo noticing me. The ship stood about a mile and a half from us, and with the first dawn of day the firing began afresh. The moment could not be far off when, the *Nautilus* attacking its adversary, my companions and myself should forever leave this man. I was preparing to go down to remind them, when the second mounted the platform, accompanied by several sailors. Either Captain Nemo did not or would not see them. Some steps were taken which might be called the signal for action. They were very simple. The iron balustrade around the platform was lowered, and the lantern and pilot cages were pushed within the shell until they were flush with the deck. The long surface of the steel cigar no longer offered a single point to check its manoeuvres. I returned to the saloon. The *Nautilus* still floated; some streaks of light were filtering through the liquid beds. With the undulations of the waves, the windows were brightened by the red streaks of the rising sun, and this dreadful day of 2 June had dawned.

'My friends,' said I, 'the moment is come. One grasp of the hand, and may God protect us!'

Suddenly an explosion took place. The compressed air blew up her decks, as if the magazines had caught fire. Then the unfortunate vessel sank more rapidly. Her topmast, laden with victims, now appeared; then her spars, bending under the weight of men; and, last of all, the top of her mainmast. Then the dark mass disappeared; and with it, the dead crew, drawn down by the strong eddy.

I turned to Captain Nemo. That terrible Avenger, a perfect archangel of hatred, was still looking. When all was over, he turned to his room, opened the door, and entered. I followed him with my eyes. On the end wall beneath his heroes, I saw the portrait of a woman, still young, and two little children. Captain Nemo looked at them for some moments, stretched his arms towards them, and, kneeling down, burst into deep sobs.

The panels had closed on this dreadful vision, but light had not returned to the saloon: all was silence and darkness within the *Nautilus*. At wonderful speed, a hundred feet beneath the water, it was leaving this desolate spot. *Where was it going?* To the north or south? Where was the man flying to after such dreadful retaliation? I had returned to my room, where Ned and Conseil had remained silent enough. I felt an insurmountable horror for Captain Nemo.

One morning I had fallen into a heavy sleep towards the early hours, a sleep both painful and unhealthy, when I suddenly awoke. Ned Land was leaning over me, saying, in a low voice, 'We are going to fly.' I sat up.

'When shall we go?' I asked.

'Tonight. All inspection on board the *Nautilus* seems to have ceased. All appear to be stupefied. You will be ready, sir?'

'Yes, where are we?'

'In sight of land. I took the reckoning this morning in the fog—twenty miles to the east.'

'What country is it?'

'I do not know but, whatever it is, we will take refuge there.'

'Yes, Ned, yes. We will fly tonight, even if the sea should swallow us up.'

'The sea is bad, the wind violent, but twenty miles in that light boat of the *Nautilus* does not frighten me. Unknown to the crew, I have been able to procure food and some bottles of water.'

'I will follow you.'

'But,' continued the Canadian, 'if I am surprised, I will defend myself; I will force them to kill me.'

'We will die together, friend Ned.'

I had made up my mind to all. The Canadian left me. I reached the platform, on which I could with difficulty support myself against the shock of the waves. The sky was threatening; but, as land was in those thick brown shadows, we must fly. I returned to the saloon, fearing and yet hoping to see Captain Nemo, wishing and yet not wishing to see him. What could I have said to him? Could I hide the involuntary horror with which he inspired me? No. It was better that I should not meet him face to face; better to forget him.

I dressed myself in sturdy sea clothing. I collected my notes, placing them carefully about me. My heart beat loudly. I could not check its pulsations. Certainly, my trouble and agitation would have betrayed me to Captain Nemo's eyes.

In desperation, I rushed through the library, mounted the central staircase, and, following the upper flight, reached the boat. I crept through the opening, which had already admitted my two companions.

'Let us go! Let us go!' I exclaimed.

'Directly!' replied the Canadian.

The orifice in the plates of the *Nautilus* was first closed, and fastened down by means of a false key, with which Ned Land had provided himself; the opening in the boat was also closed. The Canadian began to loosen the bolts which still held us to the submarine boat.

Suddenly a noise was heard. Voices were answering each other loudly. What was the matter? Had they discovered our flight? I felt Ned Land slipping a dagger into my hand.

'Yes,' I murmured, 'we know how to die!'

The Canadian had stopped in his work. But one word many times repeated, a dreadful word, revealed the cause of the agitation spreading on board the *Nautilus*. It was not us the crew were looking after!

'The maelstrom! The maelstrom!'

Could a more dreadful word in a more dreadful situation have sounded in our ears!

We were then upon the dangerous coast of Norway. Was the *Nautilus* being drawn into this gulf at the moment our boat was going to leave its sides? We knew that at the tide the pent-up waters between the islands of Ferroe and Loffoden rush with irresistible violence, forming a whirlpool from which no vessel ever escapes. From every point of the horizon enormous waves were meeting, forming a gulf justly called the 'Navel of the Ocean,' whose power of attraction extends to a distance of twelve miles. There, not only vessels, but whales were sacrificed, as well as white bears from the northern regions.

It was there that the *Nautilus*, voluntarily or involuntarily, had been run by the captain.

It was describing a spiral, the circumference of which was lessening by degrees, and the boat, which was still fastened to its side, was carried along with giddy speed. I felt that sickly giddiness which arises from long-continued whirling round.

We were in dread. Our horror was at its height, circulation had stopped, all nervous influence was annihilated, and we were covered with cold sweat, like a sweat of agony! And what noise around our frail bark! What roaring repeated by the echo miles away! What an uproar was that of the waters broken on the sharp rocks at the bottom, where the hardest bodies are crushed, and trees worn away, 'with all the fur rubbed off,' according to the Norwegian phrase!

What a situation to be in! We rocked frightfully. The *Nautilus* defended itself like a human being. Its steel muscles cracked. Sometimes it seemed to stand upright, and we with it!

'We must hold on,' said Ned, 'and look after the bolts. We may still be saved if we stick to the *Nautilus*.'

He had not finished the words, when we heard a crashing noise, the bolts gave way, and the boat, torn from its groove, was hurled like a stone from a sling into the midst of the whirlpool.

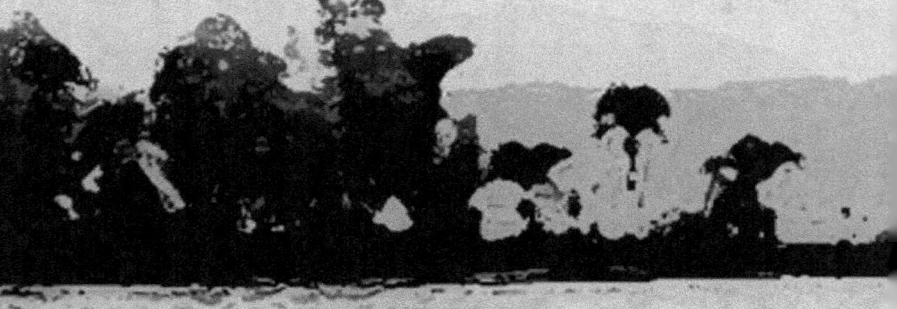

My head struck on a piece of iron, and with the violent shock I lost all consciousness.

Thus ends the voyage under the seas. What passed during that night—how the boat escaped from the eddies of the maelstrom—how Ned Land, Conseil, and myself ever came out of the gulf, I cannot tell.

But when I returned to consciousness, I was lying in a fisherman's hut, on the Loffoden Isles. My two companions, safe and sound, were near me holding my hands. We embraced each other heartily.

At that moment, we could not think of returning to France. The means of communication between the north of Norway and the south were rare. And I was therefore obliged to wait for the steamboat running monthly from Cape North.

And, among the worthy people who have so kindly received us, I revise my record of these adventures once more. Not a fact has been omitted, not a detail exaggerated. It is a faithful narrative of this incredible expedition in an element inaccessible to man, but to which progress will one day open a road.

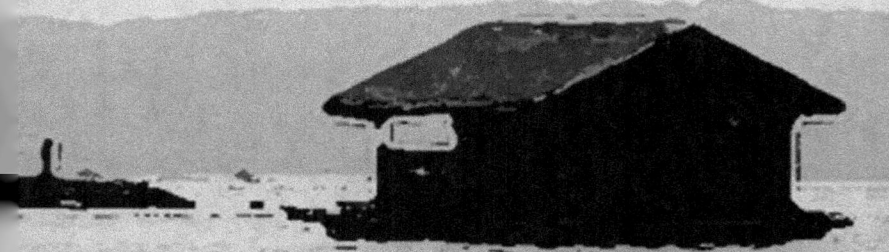

Shall I be believed? I do not know. And it matters little, after all. What I now affirm is, that I have a right to speak of these seas, under which, in less than ten months, I have crossed 20,000 leagues in that submarine tour of the world, which has revealed so many wonders.

Will the waves one day carry to him this manuscript containing the history of his life? Shall I ever know the name of this man? Will the missing vessel tell us by its nationality that of Captain Nemo?

I hope so. And I also hope that his powerful vessel has conquered the sea at its most terrible gulf, and that the *Nautilus* has survived where so many other vessels have been lost! If it be so — if Captain Nemo still inhabits the ocean, his adopted country, may hatred be appeased in that savage heart! May the contemplation of

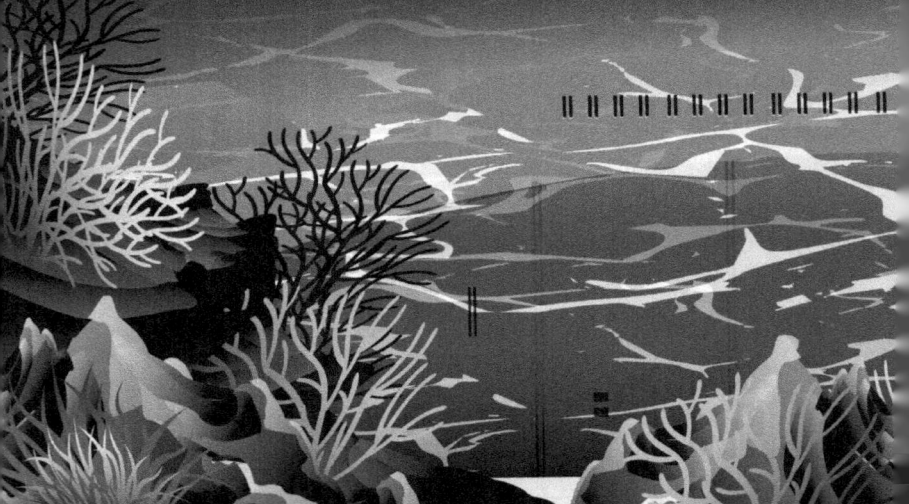

so many wonders extinguish forever the spirit of vengeance! May the judge disappear and the philosopher continue the peaceful exploration of the sea! If his destiny be strange, it is also sublime. Have I not understood it myself? Have I not lived ten months of this unnatural life? And to the question asked by Ecclesiastes 3,000 years ago, 'That which is far off and exceeding deep, who can find it out?' two men alone of all now living have the right to give an answer—

CAPTAIN NEMO AND MYSELF.

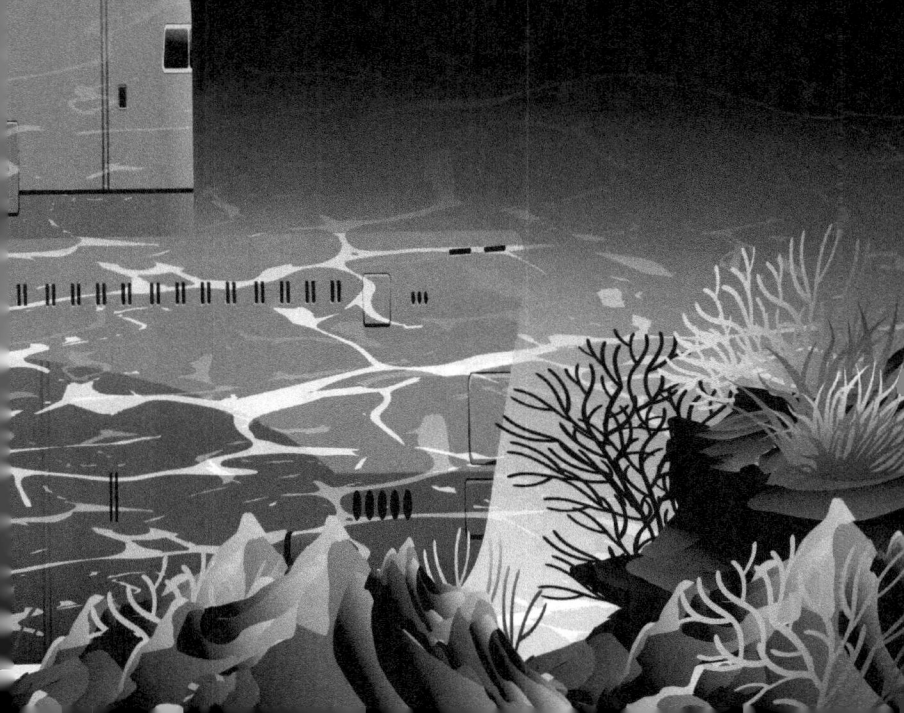

Other Titles in the Series

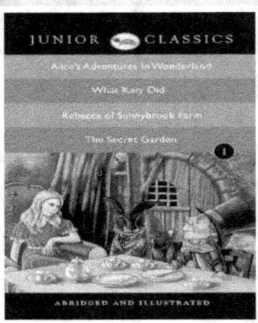

JUNIOR CLASSICS — 1
- Alice's Adventures in Wonderland
- What Katy Did
- Rebecca of Sunnybrook Farm
- The Secret Garden

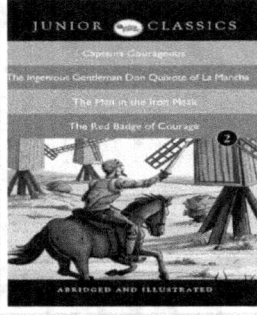

JUNIOR CLASSICS — 2
- Captains Courageous
- The Ingenious Gentleman Don Quixote of La Mancha
- The Man in the Iron Mask
- The Red Badge of Courage

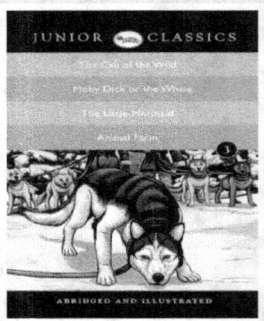

JUNIOR CLASSICS — 3
- The Call of the Wild
- Moby Dick or the Whale
- The Little Mermaid
- Animal Farm

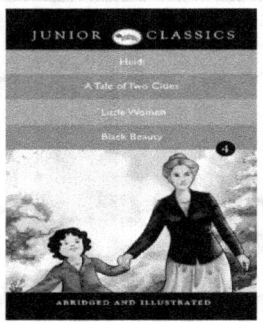

JUNIOR CLASSICS — 4
- Heidi
- A Tale of Two Cities
- Little Women
- Black Beauty

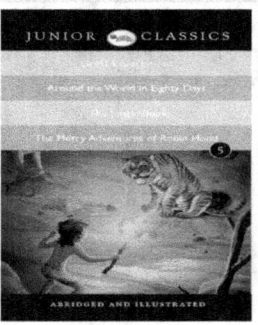

JUNIOR CLASSICS — 5
- Gulliver's Travels
- Around the World in Eighty Days
- The Jungle Book
- The Merry Adventures of Robin Hood

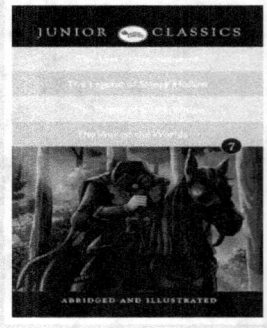

JUNIOR CLASSICS — 6
- The Adventures of Tom Sawyer
- The League of Sherlock Holmes
- The Wizard of Oz
- The War of the Worlds

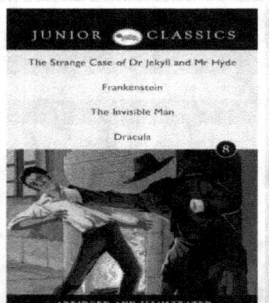

JUNIOR CLASSICS — 8
- The Strange Case of Dr Jekyll and Mr Hyde
- Frankenstein
- The Invisible Man
- Dracula

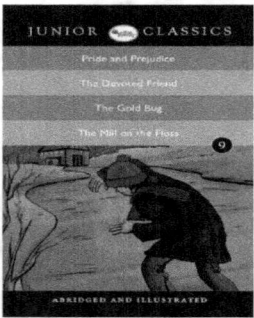

JUNIOR CLASSICS — 9
- Pride and Prejudice
- The Devoted Friend
- The Gold Bug
- The Mill on the Floss

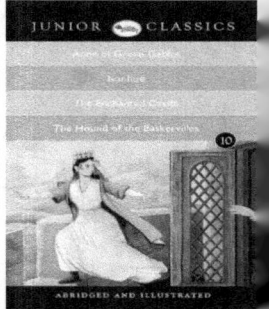

JUNIOR CLASSICS — 10
- Anne of Green Gables
- Ivanhoe
- The Brickyard Creek
- The Hound of the Baskervilles

www.ingramcontent.com/pod-product-compliance
Lightning Source LLC
Chambersburg PA
CBHW071211240526
45470CB00018B/1716